A Simple Wedding

The Spirit of Simple Living®

A Simple Wedding

A Faith-Filled Guide to Enjoying a Stress-Free Wedding

Sharon Hanby-Robie

GuidepostsBooks™
New York, New York

A Simple Wedding

ISBN-13: 978-0-8249-4713-2

ISBN-10: 0-8249-4713-4

Published by GuidepostsBooks

16 East 34th Street, New York, New York 10016

www.guidepostsbooks.com

Distributed by Ideals Publications, a Guideposts company

535 Metroplex Drive, Suite 250, Nashville, Tennessee 37211

GuidepostsBooks, Ideals and *The Spirit of Simple Living* are registered trademarks of Guideposts, Carmel, New York.

ACKNOWLEDGMENTS

Every attempt has been made to credit the sources of copyrighted material used in this book. If any such
acknowledgment has been inadvertently omitted or miscredited, receipt of such information would be appreciated.

Scripture quotations marked (AMP) are taken from *The Amplified Bible,* © 1965 by Zondervan Publishing
House. All rights reserved.

Scripture quotations marked (CEV) are taken from the *Holy Bible,* Contemporary English Version. NT
copyright © American Bible Society, 1991.

Scripture quotations marked (KJV) are taken from *The King James Version of the Bible.*

Scripture quotations marked (NIV) are taken from *The Holy Bible, New International Version.* Copyright ©
1973, 1978, 1984 International Bible Society. Used by permission of Zondervan Bible Publishers.

Scripture quotations marked (NLT) are taken from the *Holy Bible,* New Living Translation. Copyright ©
1996. Used by permission of Tyndale House Publishers, Inc., Wheaton, Illinois 60189. All rights reserved.

Library of Congress Cataloging-in-Publication Data

Hanby-Robie, Sharon.
  A simple wedding : a faith-filled guide to enjoying a stress-free wedding /
by Sharon Hanby-Robie.
    p. cm. -- (The spirit of simple living)
  ISBN 978-0-8249-4713-2
  1. Marriage--Religious aspects--Christianity. 2. Weddings. 3. Weddings--
Planning--Handbooks, manuals, etc. 4. Wedding etiquette--Handbooks,
manuals, etc. I. Title.
  BV835.H36 2007
  265'.5--dc22
                                    2006024516

Cover photograph © Stockbyte/SuperStock

Inside back flap photograph © Mark Thomas/Foodpix/jupiterimages

Author photograph by Lynn Noble

Cover and interior design by Marisa Jackson

Printed and bound in Italy

1 3 5 7 9 10 8 6 4 2

Contents

Introduction

You're getting married! What an exciting time this is. It's the beginning of a whole new life. With any new adventure there are plans to make, provisions to consider and a bit of nervous anticipation as well. That's okay—it's perfectly normal to feel both excited and anxious at the same time.

I hope to help you plan the best wedding you can imagine, and I want you to enjoy the process as much as possible. But most important, I want you, your family and your guests to simply have a fine time on your wedding day. The task of planning a wedding is not for the fainthearted. You will soon, if not already, realize that everyone has an opinion to share and expectations to express of what he or she thinks you should do. At times, you may feel as though you are being pushed and pulled in many directions at once. Let me again reassure you that this is all normal. There may be crying, even heated debates and an occasional temper-tantrum party but take it in stride—it's part of the wonderful process.

The reality is that planning a wedding is an enormous undertaking because it includes enormous responsibilities. Your marriage will unite two families forever. That is no easy feat. But don't lose heart just yet; I am going to walk you through as many of the details as I can, offering both practical and spiritual advice on how to make this adventure as simple—and personally satisfying—as possible.

As you read, I hope you will discover which size, style and budget best suits your wedding celebration dreams. I hope you will find good advice for choosing the perfect wedding dress, cake and honeymoon. But above all, I hope you are able to find peace and God's inspiration.

—*Sharon Hanby-Robie*

A Simple Wedding

The Anticipation of a Perfect Day

CREATING A UNION through marriage can be a challenge. Yet harmony can begin the moment you start planning your wedding because God is present to help you. After all, the first miracle that Christ ever performed was at a wedding when He turned water into wine, and His blessing will turn ordinary traditions into rich, momentous expressions of your love for each other. So invite God to guide you through the engagement and the wedding. As you read Part One, He will inspire you with many ideas for your upcoming day of celebration. Get your journal and make notes as we consider together this important day of your life.

A Christian Marriage

For this cause shall a man leave his father and mother,
and shall be joined unto his wife, and they two
shall be one flesh. This is a great mystery:
but I speak concerning Christ and the church.

—EPHESIANS 5:31–32 (KJV)

Marriage is a divine institution, intended—in the case of Christians—to demonstrate to the world the love that Christ has toward His bride, the church. Yet modern society sometimes challenges the definition of marriage, questioning who should be allowed to marry whom and whether marriage is even necessary between cohabiting partners. But regardless of how the contemporary culture chooses to define marriage, God's Word on the subject remains the same—marriage, like communion, is intended to represent a grand and fundamental plan with an eternal purpose.

The roles of husbands and wives, then, are not culturally determined, but divinely commanded. The spiritual union of two believers becoming one through marriage is a mystery that should be honored by the community. We honor this mysterious joining with a Christian ceremony that features not only the public avowal of our intentions, but also creates an opportunity for the community to lovingly support our commitments to each other. And believe me, all married couples can certainly use whatever support they can get.

> A wedding creates an opportunity for the community to support a couple's commitment to each other.

The image of the bride and groom, side by side, provides a marvelous symbol of how Christ stands beside the church. But we need to remember that Christ is perfect, and we are not. Christ loves us perfectly; we love others imperfectly. I relate to what Douglas J. Brouwer, author of *Beyond "I Do": What Christians Believe About Marriage*, says: "Becoming married takes time. It doesn't happen on the wedding day." I wish someone had warned my husband Dave and me about this. We were married about two weeks when Dave's brother asked him how married life was going. There was dead silence.

It does take time and a lot of work to make a marriage truly representative of the relationship that Christ offers to His Church. Dave and I really struggled those first two weeks (and the next two years) to learn how to live together in harmony. Dave had the idea that once we were married we would be more than symbiotic. He thought we would automatically be tired, hungry and so on, at exactly the same time. He thought that if he was ready to go to bed at 9:00 PM, I would be ready too. When he explained that he needed absolute silence to sleep, I bought him a pair of earplugs. Harmony in marriage can be a challenge. Dave thought *I* was quite the challenge. But the Holy Spirit worked His miracle, and now, ten years later, we have a good marriage.

Over time, as we learn to relate in unique and unconditionally loving ways toward each other, God's grace becomes visible in marriage. Michael Schevack, author of *Adam and Eve: Marriage Secrets from the Garden of Eden*, says, "When you begin to relate as males and females according to your supernatural image, you move past the popular illusions and begin to pay attention to what is essential, spiritual, eternal and even holy about your mate."

Rick Warren, author of *The Purpose Driven Life*, says that marriage is an opportunity for us to develop true intimacy and authenticity with another. That intimacy and unconditional love provides a safe environment for us to nurture and develop into the people God wants us to be. It is also where we can best develop our God-given gifts and abilities. I know that I would never have accomplished the things I have without the support and encouragement of my husband. Without Dave, I would have been afraid to take the risks necessary to achieve my goals. I would have been afraid to take the leaps of faith that God wanted me to take in order to continue to grow.

> Over time, God's grace becomes visible in a marriage.

SO WHY SHOULD WE MARRY?

Marriage helps us to gradually become the individuals God created us to be—not codependent, but loving, interdependent people who express His love by caring for each other. God said, "It is not good for the man to be alone. I will make a companion who will help him" (Genesis 2:18 NLT). The Hebrew word for help is *ezer*, which means "to protect or aid." It is the same word used in Psalm 33:20, which says that the Lord is our *help* and our shield. God's love for us is our model for marriage; we are to protect and aid each other as we strive to live as Christ instructed.

In this sense, marriage is a redemptive relationship. Ruth Muzzy and R. Kent Hughes, authors of *The Christian Wedding Planner*, say, "Three words help us understand Christ's redemptive love for the church: incarnation, death and intercession.

Through marriage, Christians are meant to experience something of each of these three elements, thus becoming more like Christ."

God incarnated in Jesus when He came to earth as a human (see John 1). Because Christ became flesh, He experienced everything that we experience: temptation, joy, pain and weakness—the whole realm of human experience. He knows what we are capable of doing, and yet He calls us to live as one in our marriage in such a way that we understand and feel what our spouses are living through.

Just as Christ died for us, we too have the opportunity in marriage to give up our own desires for the sake of the other. Marriage, unlike a casual friendship, provides a unique opportunity that makes possible truly intimate prayer for our spouse. Christ continually prayed for His bride, the church, acting as its intercessor. We are more than partners; we are intercessors for our spouses' needs.

Marriage as designed by God is meant to offer us one of the best environments for becoming all that God wants us to be. Sometimes that means allowing our mates to help God hone us into shape. Gary Thomas asks the question in his book *Sacred Marriage*, "What if God designed marriage to make us holy more than to make us happy?" This interesting question is worth remembering when your sweetheart is not meeting your blissful expectations. Obviously, God had a deeper meaning in mind when He created the institution of marriage. As we face each other's daily actions and needs, we must also come to face our own individual character flaws. And we are reminded to administer a good dose of grace and spiritual discipline to both our mates and ourselves.

SIMPLICITY MADE SIMPLE

TO BEST PREPARE for your wedding day, recognize that God wants you to go beyond having a superficial relationship with Him or your spouse. Having a good marriage relationship means first having a good relationship with your Creator. That means you must be willing to admit your hurts, fears, doubts and weaknesses, first to God and then to your fiancé. It is only when you allow God to go deep into the hidden parts of your heart that you can finally let someone else share those intimate feelings too.

REALIZE THAT YOU AND YOUR FUTURE SPOUSE DON'T HAVE TO AGREE on everything—your differences will complement each other—but you must agree on the important issues. Commitment to God and to each other is critical. Sharing the same expectations of marriage and agreeing on major life decisions, such as whether or not to have children and how much time to spend with family and friends, is also essential. I know a woman who recently married and wants to have children, but her husband (who is older than she) does not want children. She believes that she will be able to change his mind about this now that they are married. This is not only unrealistic but it is also unfair to him.

Your marriage is designed for **THE MISSION OF SERVING GOD'S PURPOSE** for both your life and His plan for the church. Ephesians 2:10 (CEV) says, "God planned for us to do good things and to live as he has always wanted us to live. That's why he sent Christ to make us what we are." Rick Warren writes, "We serve God by serving others, and we serve God by serving our spouse. God shapes us for service through a variety of methods, including our spiritual gifts, our passions, our abilities, our personality and our experiences." Sometimes our service to God requires getting through difficult phases in our marriages. Excessive planning and fretting over the details of a wedding can impose unnecessary strain on the beginning of a marriage, unless you decide simply to trust that God will make everything come together beautifully on your special day.

Marriage is a selfless situation that compels each of us to face our own selfishness daily; it teaches us to **SEE THE NEEDS OF OTHERS.** With the help of the Holy Spirit, marriage is an opportunity to view life through someone else's eyes. As you make plans for your wedding, practice seeing your future mate as God sees him. Ask God to help you be sensitive to what your spouse would like to include in the ceremony. Don't exclude your fiancé from the wedding plans—he will have wonderful suggestions that will enhance, and even simplify, your special day. Prayer is an integral part of good planning. It took me a long time to stop praying for God to make my husband into something I wanted him to be and instead pray for God to make him into the man God wants him to be. Once I understood that Dave was designed specifically for me, I truly began to enjoy God's plan for our relationship. Knowing God has a greater purpose for our marriage made it possible for me to enjoy Dave's character traits, good and bad, without trying to change him, and to simply love him just as God loves him. As you prepare for your union, take pleasure in the discovery of whom God has designed your spouse to be.

Lord, I trust that Your purpose for igniting love
between my fiancé and me is greater
than I understand presently. As we plan for
our wedding day, keep me focused on
the simple truth that You will be present to
help us enjoy all that this day is meant to represent. Amen.

You're Engaged!

I will betroth you to me forever;

I will betroth you in righteousness and justice,

in love and compassion. I will betroth you in faithfulness,

and you will acknowledge the Lord.

—HOSEA 2:19–20 (NIV)

This promise from God to His chosen people is a beautiful model to follow regarding your own engagement for marriage. God promises Israel that she will be betrothed to Him *forever*. The significant commitments in His promise to His bride are: "righteousness and justice," which indicate the legal standards required; "love and compassion," which express God's emotional concern for His bride; and "faithfulness." God is always faithful and wants us to be faithful to Him as well. This promise also asks that we *acknowledge* the Lord.

At the time of your engagement, it is important for you as a couple to acknowledge that God has a plan for your relationship. Determine together to follow God's plan for your lives and invite Him to be the central part of both your engagement and marriage.

Perhaps you and your fiancé have already agreed to marry each other through ongoing discussions, but creating a special "proposal" memory that you will have for the rest of your lives is really very nice. If your moment of commitment to each other can't be defined by a certain date and time, get your sweetie to bend a knee and "officially" ask for your hand in marriage.

> Decide who ought to be told first before announcing the news of your engagement.

Just as God's promise of eternal betrothal between Him and His people conveys a beautiful relationship, your time of engagement promises your commitment to your upcoming marriage. Once engaged, I'm sure you will be eager to share with others the excitement that you are feeling. However, what you may not realize is that *how* you announce your engagement and the order in which you tell people may affect your extended relationships in unexpected ways. Following a few simple courtesies will keep your good news celebrated without unforeseen complications.

Good news travels quickly, so before you tell the first person you see, decide who ought to be told first. For example, are your parents traditionalists who expect your fiancé to ask them for your hand in marriage? If so, then honor them with this simple act and by telling them of your plans before you announce your engagement to others. It may seem sentimental and out of fashion, but it sets the tone for all the rest of your wedding plans. That single act of respect establishes a bond between your fiancé and your father—and that is important.

You may be asking, "What if my father/parents don't like my fiancé or even know that we are serious?" If your family isn't thrilled about your choice of mate, or they are not expecting this good news, break it to them gently and be prepared for their objections. The key here is to handle the situation with love and tact. Certainly, you have a right to choose whom you want to marry; but if your family is not thrilled with your choice, it's going to make life a bit more difficult.

Christians live their lives in ways that win others for Christ simply by the way they live. The best answer to your family's objections is for you and your fiancé to continually show loving-kindness toward your family and pray for the Holy Spirit to soften their hearts. But it is still important that you at least ask for your father's blessing. How he chooses to respond is up to him.

Both sets of parents, of course, are usually the first to be told, followed by immediate family and friends. If your parents are divorced, then first tell the parent with whom you have lived. If you live in a community far away from your parents, plan a trip home for both you and your fiancé to deliver the news. It's a wonderful opportunity for your family to get to know your fiancé.

Once both sets of parents have been told, it's time for them to get to know each other. Again, this may seem somewhat out of fashion, but in the long run, creating a strong family bond on both sides is important to establishing a secure and happy home. It's traditional for the groom's parents to make the call to the bride's parents and introduce themselves. However, don't stand on formality—someone, make the call! If your parents are divorced, then the parent(s) who raised each of you should meet first.

NOW SPREAD THE WORD

When it comes to making a formal announcement of an engagement, some couples are forgoing the traditional newspaper notice and instead creating their own wedding Web page, which also allows them to update guests about developing plans. Sometimes the Web page even includes personal/romantic stories. If you choose to go the more conventional route, then a formal engagement announcement is usually made through a newspaper circulated at a location where you and your fiancé live as well as in both sets of parents' hometown papers.

This is one of the most exciting times of your life and it seems like everyone wants to share in your good news. A little time and effort in planning your engagement will go a long way in bonding your extended families, as it did for my friend Cris's family. She was surprised by a phone call from her daughter's boyfriend Matt, asking if he could visit her and her husband during Christmas break when their daughter Erin would be away. When she told her husband of the intended date, he raised his eyebrows and said, "What do you think he wants?" Cris said she hoped he wanted to discuss his desire to marry their daughter.

> Creating a Web page offers an alternative to the traditional newspaper announcement.

Cris had noticed how happy Erin was when she was with Matt. Cris enjoyed the fact that Matt filled the house with laughter whenever he came to visit. She also knew that Erin wouldn't want her to embarrass Matt with silly questions, so Cris speculated how the conversation might go and what she should say if Matt really did ask to marry their daughter. Cris decided to simply ask him to share why he loved her daughter.

The day for Matt's visit finally arrived, and Erin's parents invited him into their living room. Cris could tell that Matt was more excited than nervous as she watched him verbally unfold his reason for coming. Without any prompting, he told Cris and her husband Jim all the reasons why he admired their daughter. He said that he loved her imagination and joy of life. He loved that she made him feel courageous, as though they could go anywhere in the world, and as long as they were together, they would be okay.

Matt then told them of his plans to ask Erin to marry him on the following Saturday, saying he hoped they would be pleased and asking if they would decorate her room with Christmas lights while he took Erin to dinner. He wanted her to feel like a princess when she came home that night. Since Cris had only prepared *one* question to ask him, she was left speechless by the perfection of his delivery.

Fortunately, she remembered her husband had something warm and encouraging to say to the worthy young man in pursuit of his daughter.

When the day of engagement arrived, Matt picked up Erin and took her out for a well-planned evening of dinner and a quick stop at a movie house where a big poster was taped to a wall that featured the two of them about to appear in a romantic love story. Then he took her to a church that had decorated a garden bridge with Christmas lights. While standing on the bridge he plugged in another set of lights that read "Marry Me." Then he kneeled down and declared his love for her.

Later, after Matt brought Erin home happily waving her beautiful ring, Cris and Jim reminisced about how wonderful it was to be a part of this magical night.

Cris said, "I'm so glad he included us by asking our permission first."

Jim smiled and corrected her, "He didn't ask our permission, he simply told us of his intentions."

Cris thought Matt's approach might be even better. He had honored the idea of tradition while artistically crafting it to fit his own design. She knew her imaginative daughter had found a good match.

SIMPLICITY MADE SIMPLE

PRAY TOGETHER AS YOU PLAN YOUR FUTURE. Your time of engagement is truly the beginning of the rest of your shared lives. If you are not already in a Bible study group, this is a good time to join one—the same one. Establishing a strong commitment to pray together and for each other is a great way of ensuring that going to God will be your first course taken, whether to praise Him for the joys He brings to you or to enlist Him in the struggles you might face.

View your engagement as a season for growth. The months preceding your wedding day are a fine time to **LEARN ALL YOU CAN** to make your marriage a solid one. Reading a book together and discussing it is a wonderful way to grow as a couple and to deepen your understanding of each other's point of view. There are numerous books available for newlyweds. Here are a couple of my favorites: *Ten Commandments of Marriage: The Do's and Don'ts for a Lifelong Covenant* by Ed Young, and *The Five Love Languages: How to Express Heartfelt Commitment to Your Mate* by Gary Chapman.

Make **THE FIRST MEETING OF YOUR PARENTS** as enjoyable as possible. Some professionals suggest planning an interactive event, such as a barbecue or clambake or even a sports game, to encourage conversation. This also offers enough distractions to limit the uncomfortable moments of silence. If instead you choose to meet at a restaurant, select a lively place over a terribly quiet one. Pay for the whole meal if you are in a financial position to do so. If not, be sure that everyone understands that each couple will be responsible for their own meals. Also, make reservations at a restaurant that will accept separate checks. If you prefer to have dinner at either of your parents' homes, bring a gift or contribute to the evening's menu and offer to help clean up.

BE PREPARED TO ANSWER MANY QUESTIONS. Once you announce your engagement, the excitement of making wedding plans bubbles over. Everyone will have lots of questions: How big a wedding? Where will the ceremony be held? Mom will want to know what kind of dress she should wear. When is the date? Don't let the excitement stress you out. Instead, practice your answers in advance. Let it go something like this: "Give me a chance to climb down off my cloud and catch my breath, and then I will make these decisions. For now, I am simply going to enjoy the moment." If subtlety doesn't work on your family, then respectfully ask them to back off for a few weeks.

Throw a party and let the world know your plans. The purpose of an engagement party is to **SHARE YOUR NEWS** with your future wedding guests. Etiquette says the event should be scheduled about three months after you become engaged. Only those you plan to invite to your wedding should be asked to come to the engagement party. That is, unless you plan to have a very small wedding. In that case, make it clear to everyone at the engagement party that your wedding will be small, so that no one's feelings are hurt. Tradition holds that the bride's parents host this event. The groom's parents can have a party later, but the bride's family usually hosts the engagement party. Be sure to design the celebration in a way that everyone will be comfortable. This is not the time to make your future in-laws ill at ease. Also, remind your guests that no gifts should be brought to the engagement party, again as tradition dictates.

> Lord, I know that a wonderful future awaits
> my fiancé and me, especially because we seek
> Your wisdom for the decisions that we make.
> Help us to be sensitive to the changes we are bringing
> to our families, and help them to recognize Your plan
> to bless us throughout our union. Amen.

Premarital Mentors, Prenuptial Agreements and More!

If . . . you store up my commands within you, turning your

ear to wisdom and applying your heart to understanding, and

if you call out for insight and cry aloud for understanding,

and if you look for it as for silver and search for it as for

hidden treasure, then you will understand the fear of the

Lord and find the knowledge of God.

—PROVERBS 2:1–5 (NIV)

I am listening to the radio as I write today. It is February 13, the day before Valentine's Day, and National Public Radio is running a contest to see who their audience believes are the "top ten lovers." King Solomon is on the list! After all, he did have seven hundred wives and three hundred concubines, which leaves little doubt that he knew a bit about marriage—or did he? He was considered the wisest man who ever lived, yet the Bible says in Deuteronomy 17:14–20 that it is not wise to take many wives; and we find that Solomon's wives eventually turned his heart away from God (see 1 Kings 11:4). Obviously, acquiring wisdom and understanding is not easy. Maintaining a healthy relationship with God requires continuous pursuit, and seeking the wisdom and knowledge of God is an ongoing process. The same continuous effort is needed to create and maintain a good and happy marriage.

> ## Premarital counseling can provide a framework for creating your life together.

Simply saying *I do* will not be enough to prepare you for this rewarding commitment. Marriage today is more fragile than ever before. The divorce rate in America is now forty-eight percent of all new marriages, and it's the same for Christians. The reasons are different but the statistics are not. The number one reason cited in divorce proceedings for the general population is incompatibility. But according to research by Dr. Tom Whiteman, a Philadelphia psychologist and counselor, the leading reasons for divorce among the Christian population are adultery, abuse (including substance, physical and verbal abuse) and abandonment. In fact, some believe that Christians hang on to bad marriages longer because they feel guilty—even when there is abuse, adultery and neglect.

I don't want to scare you out of getting married; I just want you to be as prepared as you can be. I also want you to be hopeful. There is hope—and it starts with premarital counseling. Research shows that couples who participate in premarital counseling report having thirty percent stronger marriages than couples who do not seek counseling. The success of premarital counseling is so strong that some pastors simply won't marry you unless you first have counseling.

Premarital counseling provides you with a framework for how best to invest your time, energy, thoughts and prayers for your life together. It also helps you learn to appreciate the value of bringing a third-party perspective to your relationship.

Regardless of how well you think you know each other, there are still issues that you may not have thought about (or perhaps have intentionally avoided). Most couples admit that through counseling they discovered important things about themselves as well as their fiancés. Premarital counseling also teaches skills that will equip you for the challenges that marriage brings. Counselors teach couples how to communicate better and resolve conflicts. The things you will learn may seem insignificant or even silly until later in your marriage.

When Dave and I went through premarital counseling, we discovered that our ideas of a vacation were quite different. For example, Dave's idea was a simple canoe and backpack in the Canadian wilderness. My idea was a sailboat in the Caribbean. At the time of discovery, we laughed—thinking it was so cute. That was until we began to actually plan a vacation. After two bug-eaten trips to the wilderness, I said, "Enough!" We then tried sailing, but after several trips Dave finally admitted that he doesn't even like being a passenger on a keeled sailboat. This year, we went to Florida and simply relaxed on the beach together, occasionally taking a stroll along the surf. We stayed in a small "walkable" community that we both enjoyed.

SEEK HAPPILY MARRIED MENTORS

Drs. Les and Leslie Parrott, authors of several books, including *Saving Your Marriage Before It Starts*, not only believe that engaged couples should have premarital counseling, but also would like to see a national network of "marriage mentors." Marriage mentors provide helpful advice during the premarital stage and the first year of marriage. Les says, "Parents can provide valuable insight, but there's something different about spending time with couples that are not related to you. They can shoot straight with you and not feel they have anything to gain or lose, like your parents." The Parrotts believe newly married couples benefit from having access to couples who have already been through many of the things that newlyweds are about to encounter.

Pastor Robert Oglesby from South Hills Church of Christ in Abilene, Texas, has offered a mentoring program since 1995. He requires engaged couples to attend sessions that include a wide variety of topics, such as marital expectations, communication, budgeting, sexuality, weddings, honeymoons and commitment. To date, thirty-five married couples have mentored about 320 newly engaged couples. Only four of the couples who married have since divorced (a success rate of ninety-nine percent); between fifteen and twenty percent (about sixty couples) canceled their weddings entirely.

As a testimony to the benefits of marriage mentoring, nearly ninety-one percent of the premarital participants said that interacting with their mentor couple gave them a more realistic view of marriage and also had a positive effect on fostering their relationship. In addition, nearly eighty percent of the participants believed that their mentors effectively modeled how to resolve relational problems and helped them to identify issues that they had not previously discussed. An amazing ninety-five percent said they were now more concerned about their partner's happiness and had a greater awareness of their partner's needs and an increased sensitivity to each other. Who wouldn't want to be mentored if it produced those kinds of results?

Finding a mentor is an act of seeking wisdom and storing up knowledge for later use. Considering all the demands on married couples today (such as managing two careers while rearing children and paying off college debts and new mortgages, just to name a few), a mentor's support can go a long way in helping to establish communication, resolve issues, maintain mutuality and setting goals together. Without a sound foundation, it's easy to be overwhelmed, and that can only turn small problems into big ones. So don't be afraid to seek some wise advice. That's just what Carol Kuykendall did for her son Derek in order to get his marriage off to a good start.

Derek's ninety-two-year-old grandfather, whom Derek always called Papa, told his family that he and Grandma didn't feel they could make the trip from Colorado to Seattle, Washington, for his grandson's wedding. Papa explained, "We don't travel as well as we used to."

Papa had always been a special person in Derek's life, often offering his opinion with the kind of tough and tender honesty that comes from years of experience. The family felt sad about the hole Papa's absence would create, especially at the rehearsal dinner. So the week before the wedding, Derek's parents, Lynn and Carol, took Papa and Grandma Eva to lunch.

At the restaurant Carol asked, "Do you have a message you'd like us to deliver to the bride and groom at the rehearsal dinner?" Papa looked over his menu at Eva, his bride of sixty-five years, and thought for only the briefest moment. "You always hear that a successful marriage is a fifty-fifty proposition," he said, "but that formula is wrong. They'll both have to give ninety percent most of the time and then things will come out just right."

After lunch, over pie and ice cream, he added another bit of advice. "Tell them not to let the little things grow into big things."

Later, as they settled into the car and helped adjust each other's seat belts, Papa said, "There's one last thing. Tell them that in addition to loving each other, be sure they like each other."

A week later, as Lynn delivered those messages at the close of the rehearsal dinner, Carol noticed that Derek wiped his eyes as he listened to his grandfather's words. Carol knew that their beloved Papa wouldn't always be around. But even in his absence, Papa's wisdom could be carried in their hearts and passed on to others.

> Finding a mentor is an act of seeking wisdom and storing up knowledge for later use.

SIMPLICITY MADE SIMPLE

LOOK FOR A COMPREHENSIVE PREMARITAL PROGRAM. Dave and I went to Prepare-Enrich by Life Innovations, Inc. It partners with churches to present a complete program for couples that includes 165 questions on different relationship areas as well as thirty background items. It has been around for over twenty-five years and has an interactive Web site that can introduce you to the program. Samples of their statements include: "My partner has some habits I dislike." "I can share positive and negative feelings with my partner." "We have some important disagreements and they never seem to get resolved." "I have concerns about my partner's parenting skills." (You choose the answer from the following: *strongly disagree; disagree; undecided; agree; strongly agree.*) An online test can give you quick feedback to let you know areas of relationship strengths or concerns. (For more information, visit www.prepare-enrich.com.)

Premarital counseling should **FOCUS ON AT LEAST SOME OF THE FOLLOWING AREAS:** communication, conflict resolution, personality issues, financial management, sexual expectations, marital satisfaction, leisure activities, children and parenting, family and friends, expectations, idealistic distortion, role relationships and spiritual beliefs.

LEARN THE UNEXPECTED from special mentors. I recently read some interesting advice for soon-to-be-married women in *Today's Christian Woman* magazine. An article by Kelly Holmes explores the new "personal" bridal showers, where selected guests share their advice, taking seriously the instruction from Titus 2:4 that says, "Older women should train the younger women to love their husbands." They share the misconceptions they had as newlyweds and offer bits of advice. One woman for whom they held a personal bridal shower had never been to a gynecologist and wasn't sure why this was important before her wedding. They explained that some women may have conditions that could make physical intimacy difficult or put them at risk during pregnancy. One of her mentors said that she wished someone had talked to her about these personal issues before she got married. The focus of conversation at the shower remained on long-term, married intimacy as God intends it. The purpose was to encourage the bride-to-be in her future sexual relationship within a Christ-honoring atmosphere. The goal was to answer the bride-to-be's questions, prepare her for realistic expectations and inspire her toward a married lifetime of exciting and gratifying intimacy.

Along with premarital counseling, some couples are **CONSIDERING PRENUPTIAL AGREEMENTS** as well. From a biblical perspective, God does not condemn or forbid these agreements. In fact, some argue that they are very much akin to the marriage contracts of biblical times. Couples can prayerfully construct an agreement that addresses divorce, as well as death and disability. One married couple agreed before they got married that divorce would not be an option for their disagreements. Now, thirty-three years later, they are truly happy, saying they were able to find solutions to their marital conflicts without fear of abandonment because of their premarital promise to each other to avoid divorce. Financial advisers are unanimous in urging blended families (second or later marriages) to at least spell out each other's financial responsibilities in a legally binding agreement. An agreement ensures the inheritance of children from previous marriages and also protects a surviving spouse's intended assets. Harry J. Gruener, a family law attorney in Pittsburgh, Pennsylvania, says, "Young people in first marriages may also want a prenuptial agreement if one of the parties owns and is employed in a family business." He reasons that divorce or death has an impact on the integrity of the family enterprise. Marriage is built on love, honor, commitment and trust. Sometimes, a will or a trust goes hand in hand with a prenuptial agreement.

Father, I know that Your plan for marriage
is for us to make a lifelong commitment
to each other, just as You have promised
eternal love to us. Please lead us to mentors
who have learned to yield themselves to
Your grace, and give us ears to hear and understand
what they can teach us about selfless love. Amen.

Traditions and Customs

What an enormous magnifier is tradition!
How a thing grows in the human memory
and in the human imagination, when love,
worship, and all that lies in the human heart,
is there to encourage it.

—THOMAS CARLYLE, SCOTTISH HISTORIAN AND ESSAYIST (1795–1881)

I love studying the history of traditions. Wedding customs have some of the most unique beginnings. My mother is Polish, and the Poles, for example, have many beliefs that add colorful traditions to their weddings. Naturally, over time, individual families have introduced their own adaptations to make the traditions more personal. For example, the "money dance," which is very popular at Polish wedding receptions, originally positioned the maid of honor to wear an apron with pockets to hold money she collected from those who wanted to dance with the bride—and this collection would pay for the honeymoon. In our family, the bride was simply handed money from those wishing to dance with her.

The tradition of lifting the bridal veil, known as the "oczepiny ceremony," was where the bride's veil was removed as she entered the reception as a symbol of her transition to being a married woman. In our family, the veil was removed later in the midst of the reception and the apron was then placed at her waist as a symbol of her new life as a married woman.

> Today's wedding traditions and customs can be traced back to many different cultures.

Many of today's popular traditions can be traced to ancient times. The first marriages were not by choice but by capture. The legend says that when early man felt it was time to take a bride, he literally took one and carried her away to a secret place where her family could not find her. He would keep her hidden for about thirty days as the moon went through all its phases. As they hid, they drank from a fermented brew made of mead and honey; hence, the word *honeymoon*. The tradition of carrying the bride across the threshold is also tied to the same legend. A captured bride was not likely to go willingly into the bridegroom's den—so she was carried or dragged across the threshold. Another superstition held that family demons would follow the woman—so the man carried her over the threshold upon entering for the first time. After that, I guess the demons gave up.

The wearing of the wedding band on the third finger of the left hand has a number of different legends associated with it too. In ancient times it was believed that there was a vein in the third finger of the left hand that ran directly to the heart, so the ring was worn on this finger. Of course, medical science has long since disproved this theory, but we perpetuate the tradition as a symbol of our love and commitment. Another theory suggests that the bridegroom placed the ring on three of the bride's fingers consecutively in order to symbolize the Holy Trinity, finally leaving it there on the third finger.

Have you ever noticed that bridesmaids and groomsmen resemble the bride and groom a bit in terms of attire? The original idea was to confuse onlookers—especially evil wishers—and perhaps an unrequited old lover who might want to prevent the bride and groom from rejoicing "happily ever after."

Regarding the bride's attire, I thought that the white dress was to symbolize purity, right? Then I read that brides simply wore their best dresses until some time between 1499 and the late sixteenth century. The color blue is a symbol of purity. The color white symbolizes joy. Again, there are differing opinions about why we wear white. One story gives credit to Anne of Brittany for wearing a white dress in 1499. Another story credits Queen Victoria who chose to wear white over the traditional royal color of silver for her wedding in the 1840s. Now some brides wear ivory, simply because it looks better than bright white with their skin tones.

The wedding cake has always been a special part of the wedding celebration. The history of the wedding cake began in early Roman times when a thin wheat or barley loaf was broken over the bride's head at the close of the ceremony to symbolize fertility. Guests were said to scramble for the pieces of the cake and take them home as a good luck charm. Later, during the Middle Ages, it became a tradition to make the cake as tall as possible by placing many small cakes on top of each other. The bridal couple was then expected to attempt a kiss over this tower of cakes without knocking it down. Some records claim that during the reign of King Charles II of England, the baker simply added icing to the tower of cakes, and thus the modern wedding cake was born.

START A NEW WEDDING TREND

Traditions are timeless, but that doesn't mean you can't create a few of your own symbolic memories. Writer Van Varner attended a wedding with a new idea for an old tradition that made the festivities truly joyful. His story follows:

My godson Ty and his Amanda were being married in a fine old church in California's Napa Valley. The couple was standing before the altar with their attendants loyally in line and with dozens of relatives and friends sitting decorously in our pews, properly solemn, beads of perspiration forming on our brows. This, after all, was a sweltering afternoon in July.

Came time for the first hymn. *What was this?* I checked back to see if I'd read the right number. *No, that was correct.* And so we started to sing "Joy to the World." *A Christmas hymn in the middle of the summer?* Well, at least we all knew the music and the words were familiar.

Vows were exchanged, Ty and Amanda became husband and wife, and once again we picked up our hymnals. What? "Angels We Have Heard On High"? *Another* Christmas hymn?

The music began. Here was a song we not only knew but this time we were ready for it. And sing it we did, boisterously, joyfully, all together, all smiling, *Glor-or-or-oria in excelsis Deo, glor-o-or-or-ia in excelsis Deo*—praise God and hurrah for Ty and Amanda!

Later, in talking with the bride and groom, they said, "We wanted hymns that would be joyous and easy to sing. And, anyway, when was it *ever* out of season to sing gladly about the birth of the Son of God!"

Let me tell you, it's nice to have a godson who can teach his old godfather a spiritual lesson from time to time.

SIMPLICITY MADE SIMPLE

TRY SOMETHING OLD, SOMETHING NEW, SOMETHING BORROWED AND SOMETHING BLUE. ADD A SILVER SIXPENCE IN YOUR SHOE. This little rhyme that originated in Victorian times was designed to ward off evil spirits. Something *old* symbolizes the sense of continuity or the passing down of good fortune. Something *new* symbolizes that marriage is a transition to adulthood and to the bright and happy new future you will have together. Something *borrowed* was usually a valued item from the bride's family. It was to symbolize prosperity in the new union—but it would only bring good fortune if it were returned to the family. Something *blue* came from the representation that blue symbolizes purity, constancy and fidelity. In an ancient tradition in Israel, blue was placed on the hem of the bride's dress. In other cultures a blue ribbon was worn in the bride's hair as a symbol of fidelity. The placing of a silver sixpence in the bride's shoe was to ensure wealth. Today, many a bride simply slips a penny in her shoe.

DON'T FEEL PRESSURED TO INCLUDE EVERY TRADITION. Instead, consider using a few old traditions and creating your own new tradition as well. After all, the timeless traditions were once all new too. Or try borrowing some traditions from your family's ethnic background or find some others that interest you. For example, did you know that in Finland instead of throwing a bouquet to the single women, the bride is blindfolded and the single women gather in a circle around her? As music plays the bride slowly turns in one direction while the circle of women walks in the other. When the music stops, the bride simply walks forward and the lucky single gal who is directly in front of her receives the bouquet.

CREATE YOUR OWN THEME FOR YOUR WEDDING and incorporate it into traditional ideas. For example, if you love the beach, consider using shells as a decorative and symbolic accent. Shells represent baptism. In a way, your marriage signifies the beginning of a new life, just as baptism does. Your ring pillow, for example, could be adorned with shells and crystals. You might also display the same accents in your bouquet and on your unity candle as well.

Don't throw rice. In fact, most churches won't allow it. Instead, **CONSIDER SOME ENVIRONMENTALLY FRIENDLY PRODUCTS.** Try Eco-fetti. It is biodegradable confetti, perfect for tossing over the newlyweds without worry of harming the environment. This confetti is water-soluble and it disintegrates when wet. Or throw birdseed and leave a little meal for your feathered friends. However, check with your church or other house of worship first, because some don't allow birdseed either. If they say no, then let the bubbles and the sound of jingling fill your wedding ceremony with decorated jars of bubble and bell favors. A custom gift tag, imprinted with names of the bridal couple and the event date, can be attached to miniature gold or silver bells.

Lord, as we plan our ceremony, help us to embrace the real purpose of each tradition that we include. Let our wedding become testimony of Your everlasting love for us, and may the mystery be revealed that true love is God at work between two people. Amen.

Your Wedding, Your Way

Blessed are they whose ways are blameless, who walk
according to the law of the Lord. Blessed are they who keep
his statutes and seek him with all their heart.

—PSALM 119:1–2 (NIV)

It's amazing what happens the minute you announce your plans to be married. Suddenly, everyone has an opinion about what constitutes the "perfect wedding." Aunt Matilda offers her neighbor as your caterer—despite the fact that this person has never catered a wedding in her life. Mere acquaintances line up to volunteer to be in your wedding. And somehow it becomes imperative that you invite everyone—including relatives and family friends whose names you have never even heard before.

Don't let yourself become overwhelmed by all those good intentions. Take a breath and simply explain to these well-meaning people that you are not ready to make those decisions just yet. Let them know that you will consider their ideas and suggestions. Then find some time for you and your fiancé to seriously hash out what the most meaningful things are to you regarding your wedding. Your wedding is *your* special day. Therefore, it should absolutely be *your* dream of a wedding—not anyone else's.

There are a few cautions I would like to point out. This wedding of yours is going to unite two different families. The grudges and resentments that may occur as a result of your plans could last a lifetime. Only you and your fiancé can decide how much you are willing to risk versus how far you are willing to compromise on your ideal wedding plans. Psalm 119 is the longest in the Bible. This entire Psalm is a reflection on God's laws. Verses 1–16 particularly reflect on walking always in God's way. As you make your wedding plans, follow the way God would have you arrange things. Be sure that you have His priorities straight. It is only then that you can stand firmly and strongly defend your desires for your wedding.

> As you make your wedding plans, follow the way God would have you arrange things.

Most of the time, you will find that families calm down after a while and agree to most of your plans. Occasionally a young couple can find themselves in a position where they must take drastic steps in order to protect their relationship. My brother planned on getting married in April. Both he and his soon-to-be bride wanted a small, simple wedding that would only include immediate family. It wasn't long before it became apparent that some family members had a different idea about the wedding plans. Before this couple knew what was happening, the small simple wedding had ballooned into the event of the century. And it was taking a toll on their relationship. The stress and strain had them arguing with each other and with other family members. Finally, in desperation, the bride-to-be called off the engagement entirely. My brother was devastated. This was the love of his life—how could this be happening?

Thankfully, she believed that my brother was also the love of her life. So instead of continuing the battle over how to celebrate a marriage, the two of them simply slipped away and married on the same day they had originally planned—alone, without any family. A few days before, they told those of us who they knew would accept their plans without fuss. We were thrilled that they had the courage to move forward in a way that worked for them. It may seem sad that it came down to this outcome, but it was better than their not getting married at all only because the family was more intent on throwing a party than respecting the wishes of the bride and groom.

NONTRADITIONAL WEDDINGS ARE PERFECT TOO

I had a blast at my wedding. I have no regrets. Since Dave and I met at church, everyone there watched us fall in love. So naturally, they all wanted to be a part of our wedding. To accommodate, we simply let everyone who wanted to attend the church ceremony do so, then celebrated with cake and coffee in the church gymnasium. We invited forty-five of our closest family and friends to dinner and then had a big party at (what was to become) our home afterward. In fact, we even had several family members staying with us in our home. In the morning, we all had breakfast together. It was wonderful!

Of course, as with most couples, there were things that some family members "thought" we should do that we passed on. For example, since this was a second marriage for me and I was in my midforties at the time, I didn't think it appropriate to announce our engagement in the newspaper. It wasn't something I was comfortable with and it wasn't something that really mattered to Dave. I also chose not to wear a hat, even though someone thought I should. I hadn't worn a hat in years—why start on my wedding day? I wore a suit, not a gown. My husband and several other friends sang at our wedding—a bit unconventional for some folks, but absolutely perfect for us, especially considering they all have amazing voices. In fact, friends that attended said it was better than going to a Broadway show. We did things our way and we enjoyed every minute of it.

A couple I know had a Las Vegas wedding. The bride said it was the simplest wedding to plan. She made one phone call to a Vegas wedding planner and everything was taken care of. Forty of her family and friends flew out with them for the wedding. I read about a couple that didn't want a big ceremony so they chose to be married alone and then planned on having a big party a few months later to celebrate. They made family and friends feel like part of the wedding by sending each a "wedding in a box." The box contained an announcement, some photos from their ceremony, a small favor, Jordan almonds in a little tulle bundle and some confetti. What fun!

There are a lot of decisions to make when it comes to planning your wedding. By the time you finish, you'll be an expert at it. In the meantime, simply relax and enjoy the process while creating some wonderful memories. Be as flexible and accommodating as you can—take the high road as much as possible. Always remember: This is about creating an experience that symbolizes the kind of life the two of you want to share together.

SIMPLICITY MADE SIMPLE

Present a united front. M. A. Woodman of WedAlert.com says the first thing an engaged couple should do is to carefully discuss in private what is going to be negotiable and what is not. He also suggests that when the warring starts to develop into a bad memory, simply try to be "hard of listening," even if for just a while. He says, "Your only other choice is grudges among family that may last for years, or a lifetime—do you want that? Is it worth it?" **KNOW WHAT IS IMPORTANT TO YOU.** What is your vision of an ideal wedding? How flexible are you on the type of wedding you will have? How do you feel about eloping?

DECIDE WHO'S IN CHARGE. This is not only a question that should be asked between the couple, but you must consider those paying for the wedding as well. If your parents are paying, how much influence should that give them? Is it worth it? Is having your dream wedding worth paying for it yourself? How much money do you think is appropriate to spend on your wedding? Be sure that you and your fiancé have the same expectations before you let family get involved. One couple didn't want a wedding that revolved around spending tons of money simply to get some likely meaningless gifts from people they barely knew. Instead, they wanted their wedding to be more significant and reflective of their own beliefs. They handmade their own announcements and asked that people not feel obligated to give them anything but their kindest regards.

BE UP FRONT. The best way to avoid conflicts is simply to explain your expectations about your wedding to your family at the same time you announce your plans to get married. That way, *their* wedding fantasies don't have time to materialize and run wild before they know what your dream is. Don't get into huge disagreements over wedding plans. Remember that a wedding is more than a ceremony. It is about very deep issues such as money, beliefs, desires and philosophies. Don't be afraid to discuss disappointments. Your parents may have been dreaming about your wedding since you were born. Let them talk about it. Who knows, it may be possible to accommodate them and still have the ceremony you want.

> Lord, by Your Spirit, draw wedding guests to attend
> our celebration who will support us with prayer, and
> cover us with the grace of Your faith in marriage.
> Protect us from calamity or confusion, and fill the day
> with the peace of Your awesome presence. Amen.

Special Challenges: Remarriage, Interfaith Weddings and Divorced Parents

I am my beloved's, and my beloved is mine:

He feedeth among the lilies.

—SONG OF SOLOMON 6:3 (KJV)

Song of Solomon (Song of Songs) is one of the most explicit books in the Bible. Though there are disagreements about its intended purpose, most will agree that Song of Solomon tells of the love between a bridegroom and his bride. It affirms the sanctity of marriage and is the perfect picture of God's all-encompassing love for His people. His love is more than reason enough for us to commit to seeing life and marriage from His point of view.

I believe that God's view is clear in telling us to avoid being unequally yoked.

There are numerous stories throughout the Bible of interfaith marriage and the consequences thereof. There can be trouble even when the motive is "good," as depicted when King Solomon takes the daughter of the king of Egypt as his bride in order to secure peace (see 1 Kings 3:1). Marriage between royal families was common practice simply because it did bring agreement between countries. However, this alliance also initiated Solomon's downfall because it introduced idols into his country, eventually luring Solomon into idolatry.

> Interfaith marriages, remarriages and divorced parents can present special challenges when planning a wedding.

It's easy to minimize religious differences when you are in love. But these seemingly insignificant differences can have an enormous impact on your relationship with each other and with your families as the years progress. My first husband was an agnostic. When I was young, both in faith and age, I didn't see how this could be such a big deal. As is true for most people, the more mature we became the stronger our stands in our individual beliefs grew; it became more difficult for us to find common ground.

God's way is always best. He gives us standards to follow for all of life's relationships, especially marriage. If we follow His plan, even when the path is difficult, we have a mutual foundation to stand on together. Our culture today is a hodgepodge of interfaith marriages, remarriages, divorced parents, even third and fourth marriages.

When I married for the second time, my husband's family had a hard time accepting the fact that his bride was divorced. Dave had never been married so it was only natural for them to want a "new" bride for their son. However, Dave was thirty-nine years old when we married. The reality was that there were not a lot of women his age that had never been married, which leads to the discussion of the many different kinds of second marriages there can be and the challenges they can present.

The possibilities are endless when it comes to invitations, especially if you choose to design them yourself.

You may want to carry the theme of your invitations through to your programs as well.

Decide early which traditions are most meaningful to you
and your fiancé, and plan your celebration around them.

Fresh flowers make a lovely decoration for your wedding cake.

Often, one of the most meaningful moments at a reception is the bride and groom's first dance. You and your fiancé may want to consider a few dance lessons before the big day.

For example, there can be two divorced people marrying each other, a never-married person marrying a divorced person and a widowed person marrying a divorced or a never-married person. Now add to this smorgasbord those with children and those without and the menu can get very confusing. Just how do you handle such a complexity of marriages?

LOOK TO THE FUTURE, NOT TO THE PAST

First, we must all realize the background and baggage each one of us brings to the new marriage. The patterns and behaviors established in our first marriages will absolutely overflow into our new one without our even realizing it. Having realistic expectations and being able to discuss and resolve conflicts are critical to your marriage. And learning to resolve conflicts will start as you plan your wedding. Have your eyes wide open and acknowledge the trouble spots. If you anticipate, for example, that your children may have trouble accepting your new marriage, rather than ignoring this fact and hoping things won't be as bad as you expect, be frank about your concerns and don't hesitate to seek professional advice to help your family members adapt to the changes that are being made. Also be aware that simply because your fiancé doesn't have children doesn't change the fact that he will have an opinion on how to raise yours. Be forthright about potential issues and put together a realistic plan for dealing with them in an up-front manner. Being armed with facts makes us all better equipped to deal with problems as they arise.

I have a friend whose first husband was killed at a very young age in a plane crash. When she remarried she found herself fighting a "ghost." The ghost was idealized memories of her first husband. Every time her new hubby did something that upset her or that she found hard to deal with, she found herself comparing him to her late husband. My friend had to first realize that there is no such thing as a perfect mate. Then she also had to accept that her memories of her late husband were not exactly the entire truth. He had faults too, as we all do.

The reality is that second marriages present special problems both for the marriage and for the planning of the wedding. If you have a good relationship with your former in-laws, you may want them at the wedding for your children's sake. Especially if they still spend time with your children, it may help them to accept the new parent their grandchildren will have. But think about how your fiancé may feel about this. If he goes along grudgingly, it may become something that escalates into an issue later. Loyalty is obviously an essential component of a good marriage. Having allegiances and representatives from former marriages at your new wedding may not be the best way to get started. Your wedding should be the day where you and your future spouse are united in solidarity and that should take precedence over previous attachments.

SIMPLICITY MADE SIMPLE

CONFER WITH YOUR MINISTER OR OTHER RELIGIOUS LEADER. If you are an interfaith couple you may find it more difficult than you think to locate someone to perform the marriage. This is especially true if one of you is Jewish. Though most temples accept interfaith couples as part of the congregation—many will not officiate at such a union. Rabbi Barry Baron of Houston, Texas, says, "In Judaism, marriage is a holy act, or mitzvah, desirable to God and governed by Jewish law. Jewish law was conceived by my rabbinic forebears as encompassing the behavioral norms which God desires of Jews." Rabbi Baron continues, "Jewish law sanctions the marriage of Jews to each other, and as a rabbi, I feel that I can only officiate at marriages which Jewish law sanctions." Although his opinion by no means represents all rabbis, it is something that the two of you need to be prepared to deal with. Some rabbis will agree to marry interfaith couples but only if they decide to raise the children in the Jewish faith.

CONSIDER HAVING ONLY ONE FAITH REPRESENTED at your wedding. In her book, *Interfaith Wedding Ceremonies*, Joan C. Hawxhurst suggests the following: "If only one partner feels strongly about his or her religious identity, you can choose to have a wedding in only that tradition. In this case, you will need to find a representative of only one of your faith traditions." This will allow you to bypass many of the objections raised by clergy about interfaith marriages.

BALANCE BOTH RELIGIOUS TRADITIONS or have two separate ceremonies. If you are both committed to your faith, you can elect to choose a representative from each of your traditions to present your wedding. In some larger communities, you can often find Christian and Jewish clergy that have teamed up and are comfortable with such a blended ceremony. Or you can choose to have two separate ceremonies—though only one will be legally binding. For example, if you cannot find a rabbi who is willing to officiate at a dual service, perhaps your rabbi is willing to bless your marriage afterward in a smaller ceremony. A friend of mine is Catholic and her husband is Greek Orthodox, so they had two ceremonies. They married in the Catholic church first and then went to Greece for a wedding there too.

Seek "respectful presence." If your families are finding it difficult to attend an interfaith ceremony, ask them to simply **CONSIDER GIVING RESPECTFUL PRESENCE.** This is a term coined by the governing body of the Presbyterian Church's General Assembly in 1997. "Respectful presence is a way for Christians to be present with persons of other religious traditions in a variety of settings, expressing deep respect for those persons and their faith while maintaining loyalty to the Christian gospel."

Second weddings are a reason for celebration and rejoicing. However, **THE KEY IS MODERATION.** The emphasis should be on the religious aspects of your wedding ceremony, not on all the pomp and circumstance. It is acceptable for you to have bridesmaids, but it is more common to have only one or two very close friends stand with you. And certainly, children of the bride or groom should be an important part of the ceremony. As for your dress, Martha A. Woodham, author of *Wedding Etiquette for Divorced Families*, suggests that you enjoy an elegant evening dress or suit instead of a wedding gown with a train.

CONSULT WITH YOUR CHURCH OR OTHER PLACE OF WORSHIP. Some churches have very specific rules regarding what is and is not acceptable for a second marriage. Many do not allow a long white gown with train. Some say no to a veil. Remember that a large number of the wedding traditions don't have a biblical foundation anyway. So do your best to honor as many of your tradition's requirements or prohibitions as you can accept.

Divorced parents can present some very tricky problems. **IF YOU OR YOUR FIANCÉ HAVE PARENTS WHO ARE DIVORCED OR REMARRIED**, you will most likely have some interesting situations to handle. Obviously, the best state of affairs would be that everyone gets along just fine and all agree to act like adults throughout the celebration. If not, there are some rules of etiquette to help you keep interactions pleasant. Head off awkwardness and stress by making up seating arrangements well in advance that put as much distance as possible between your divorced parents. Also, it may help clear the air to speak with your parents ahead of time. If someone refuses to attend if so-and-so is invited, Pamela Hill Nettleton, author of *Getting Married When It's Not Your First Time*, suggests that you try to calm the storm with straight talk, such as: "This is my wedding, not your battleground. I care about each of you and want you both to be there. I'd consider it a big 'I love you' message if you'd please attend."

Dear God, it is a temptation for us to look at
the diminishing memories of our past instead
of the bright light of our future. Let the day
of our union mark a new commitment in all of us
to focus on the truth of Your promise to make
all things work together for our good as we
obediently put our hope in You. Amen.

PART TWO

A Day That Belongs to You

ENJOY YOURSELF as you choose colors and themes and even wedding guests. Keep in mind that your wedding day is about you and your groom, so whether your wedding is formal, semiformal or intimate, it will be perfect as long as it reflects your personal style. This next section is filled with information that will make upcoming decisions easier. I will even explain how to choose planners as well as how to delegate assignments to your bridesmaids if you feel overwhelmed by the planning process. So relax. No matter what you decide, come rain or come sunshine, you are about to enjoy a simply beautiful wedding day.

Your Wedding Style

Be joyful at your Feast—you, your sons and daughters, your
menservants and maidservants, and the Levites, the aliens,
the fatherless and the widows who live in your towns.

—DEUTERONOMY 16:14 (NIV)

As we study the Old Testament, we see that religious observances were punctuated by a feast and a joyful celebration. Although there were specific activities and rituals associated with the various festivals, they all included sacrifices, prayers, special meals, ceremonies and special customs. Your wedding is a very personal occasion for celebration that should reflect your hopes, dreams and beliefs. As you plan your dream wedding, you too may find that sacrifice, reflective prayer, and serious consideration to meals and ceremonial family customs will be necessary.

To simplify your plans, you must first decide what type of wedding you want: a formal, semiformal or informal wedding. Of course, your budget will greatly influence your decision. We'll talk more seriously about finances later, but at this point, you do need to have a good idea of how much you want to spend. For example, the more formal your affair, the more costly it will be by definition.

Your first decision is in choosing the type of wedding you want: formal, semiformal or informal.

A *formal* wedding means that you plan on the big shebang with all the trimmings—usually two hundred to five hundred guests and a formal wedding gown with a train and veil. It also generally means the men will be dressed in white tie or formal daywear and that there will be four or more attendants for each of you. While the bride's dress can be the same for formal daytime or formal evening, the basic formal attire for the groom and other men in the wedding party (i.e., groomsmen, ushers, fathers) changes when it's formal daytime versus formal evening. Formal daytime wear is a morning suit, which is a cutaway coat with tails, gray pinstripe trousers, gray vest, ascot or tie. Formal evening wear is "full dress," which is black tailcoat, matching black pants, white shirt, white vest and white tie. The groom and other men can wear a tuxedo instead of a morning suit for formal daytime or instead of "full dress" for formal evening. A groom can distinguish himself from the rest of the wedding party by varying an accessory such as the boutonniere, tie or vest. However, to be in totally correct dress for a formal evening wedding, there is no variation among the men. They all wear white tie and tails.

A formal wedding would also include engraved invitations and elaborate decorations with a reception at a private club or an exclusive hotel. Of course, it would have to include an orchestra for dancing as well. (I'm not making this up—this is the actual meaning of a "formal" wedding as defined by nearly every wedding etiquette book in print.)

If you can already feel the pinch on your pocketbook, then perhaps you would like to consider something a little simpler. A *semiformal* wedding has a guest list of one hundred to two hundred and fifty people. But wedding etiquette considers it to be bad taste if you wear a dress with a train at a semiformal wedding. (Who makes up these rules?) The men should wear black tie or conservative dark suits. If you are getting married in the summer, you might get away with white dinner jackets instead. The invitations can be engraved traditionally or you could have them printed on ivory or white paper instead if you are interested in saving a little money. In a semiformal wedding, you will have fewer attendants—no more than three each. And it would be okay to have a buffet or even an afternoon tea instead of a full-course, sit-down dinner. You could also get away with a small combo or even a single musician instead of a full orchestra.

My favorite wedding style is an *informal* one, because it simply allows you more flexibility to focus on what is most important to you. An informal wedding can take place anywhere you would like. A small church or chapel for fifty to one hundred of your closest friends and family can be perfect. You could wear a long or a short wedding dress or even your favorite pretty dress. Your veil shouldn't be longer than elbow length for an informal wedding. Your dress for an intimate wedding should basically reflect your own personality. If it's your first wedding, then go ahead and wear your gown. If it's a second wedding, then a street-length dress or suit makes more sense. And you should keep your attendant to one maid or matron of honor. The groom should choose just one man for his attendant as well. The men can wear dark conservative suits or black tie if they prefer. Your invitations can be whatever you like, including handwritten. A simple buffet or light lunch or even afternoon tea with finger foods can be served.

My friend Jan had an *intimate* wedding at her home when she married for the second time. It was wonderful. An intimate wedding is a charming small affair that

> An informal wedding allows for the most flexibility in planning.

can take place anywhere. Most home weddings are of this warm and personal nature, and that's just what my friend Jan had. Her ceremony was supposed to be outdoors— but it rained. So we used her back-up plan and had the ceremony in her living room in front of the fireplace.

EXPRESS YOURSELF

Now, just because "etiquette" gives all these rules and regulations regarding each type of wedding, it doesn't mean you have to follow them. Treat them as mere suggestions. As I have said, and will continue to emphasize, this is your day. That means you will take into consideration the opinions of those that matter to you, but in the end, you will go where your heart leads you to go.

The most important thing you can do is take some time to sit down with your fiancé and make a list of those things that are most essential for each of you. Determine what is negotiable and what is not. Understand that regardless of what the wedding planners and the retail and service providers want you to believe, there is no such thing as perfection on earth.

There obviously are a lot of factors that must be taken into account when deciding the type of wedding you would like to have. The location is a key decision to make. Simply said, some locations are more conducive to specific kinds of weddings than others. If you want to have the traditional, Christ-honoring ceremony in a church, then start there. My church has grown and the building is so heavily scheduled that it is very difficult for the church staff to accommodate weddings. That's sad, but it's the reality. Having a reception at our church would also be quite restricted, because caterers are only allowed to serve in the lobby café. There is little privacy in that open area, so having a reception at our church probably would not make sense.

As I mentioned earlier, Dave and I met and married in our previous church, which was much smaller, and even at a smaller church we faced some problems with their schedule. We tried six different dates and finally asked them to tell us when to show up. We wanted to wed in spring, but part of the problem was that we had an outreach to our community that included a full-length musical twice a year—one at Easter. We were both involved in the Easter musical that year. I was directing and Dave was acting and singing. Of course, with rehearsals, set building, orchestra practice, etc., having the wedding in the months preceding the musical wasn't an option. We finally settled on the week after Easter and got married in Jerusalem. (The set was still up, pillars and all—it was quite the backdrop for a wedding.)

Many of us dream about our wedding day from the time we are young. In the end, the most important thing is that we feel beautiful, honored and cherished. When my husband asked me what was my most important expectation for our ceremony, I told him it was simply to feel cherished—and that part of the planning was left up to him. He met my expectations by singing to me. I wanted the song to be a surprise, but our dearest friend suggested he sing it at the rehearsal, knowing that it would overwhelm me emotionally and make it very hard for me to regain my composure. He was right. Nonetheless, I cried at our wedding—just not uncontrollably.

SIMPLICITY MADE SIMPLE

Consider the statement you want your wedding to make. Your wedding is not just a symbol of your shared love but also an expression of your personalities and what you esteem most in your relationship. **THINK ABOUT WHAT YOU WANT YOUR CEREMONY TO SAY**. What do you want guests to remember about your wedding? Both you and your fiancé should make a list detailing the elements that are most important, identifying which are essential and which are negotiable. Remember, when it comes to compromising, the key is a win-win situation. Nancy Twigg, author of *Celebrate Simply*, suggests applying patience, persistence and creativity in devising a plan that will fulfill what both of you desire from your wedding experience. She also warns "not to lose sight of the ultimate meaning of your special day—two people in love committing their lives to each other. Ten years from now, no one will care what kind of gown you wore or if your flowers were fresh or silk."

Once the two of you know what you want, gather your family together. **SHARE YOUR PLANS WITH YOUR FAMILY** for how you want your wedding and reception to be handled. Be prepared for high emotions—the closer you get to the wedding day, the stronger they become. Acknowledge your family's feelings, but confirm your stand as well as your loyalty to family. It's normal for Mom and Dad to feel as though they are losing their little girl or boy. Let them know their help is appreciated, but gracefully assert yourself as the final decision-maker.

CONSIDER A THEME. Though not necessary, a theme can make your plans easier. Whether it's cultural, ethnic or topical, such as a beach theme, it can help you focus on style. Victorian is a very popular style for weddings. This is an especially good match if you are wearing an antique gown. Color is another important element in planning your wedding. Invitations, gowns, decorations and flower choices will all be affected by your choice of color. But before you choose, confirm that the interior decorations of your wedding reception location will work with your personal choices. Most professionals will tell you to choose your colors using the Pantone color system numbers to assure that everyone is able to identify the exact shades you prefer. The printer, the florist and the bridal shops all use this universal system. Allison Micarelli suggests restricting your color choices to five essential wedding elements to avoid overdoing it. The essential elements she suggests are attire, invitations, flowers, cake and favors. For Allison's complete article and more wedding ideas, visit www.TheKnot.com.

CHECK TO SEE IF YOUR DESIRED LOCATION HAS EVERYTHING YOU WILL NEED. One friend of mine had an untraditional wedding. He's a professional bowler so he got married at a bowling alley and had his reception there as well. Basic items like table linens, glassware and the like had to be rented from elsewhere.

TAKE ADVANTAGE OF THE MANY RESOURCES. Here is a list of just a few that I found very helpful: WeddingChannel.com, ModernBride.com and TheKnot.com. And you can always hire a wedding consultant. Just be sure that he or she belongs to The Association of Bridal Consultants. It is the only international trade association dedicated to serving the wedding profession.

> Lord, in our desire to plan a perfect day,
> keep us focused on the simple truth
> that You ordained this day in our lives
> to be a joyful, festive celebration. Amen.

Time to Talk Money

A feast is made for laughter, and wine makes life merry,

but money is the answer for everything.

—ECCLESIASTES 10:19 (NIV)

Ah . . . sometimes it does seem that having just a little more money would certainly make things easier, especially when planning an event like a wedding. In the verse from Ecclesiastes 10, Solomon is warning us of the myth that money and/or liquor are the answer to all of life's problems. The truth is that their balm is only temporary and when their positive effects wear off, reality will hit you even harder. The Bible is very clear about God's view of money. In simple terms, "It belongs to Him." You are only allowed to manage it for Him. I say this to help you get and keep a good perspective as you begin to put together a budget for your wedding. Budget? Yes, budget.

As an interior designer I had to learn to get comfortable talking about money with people from all walks and of all ages of life. You see, it is impossible for me to design a room without knowing how much money there is to spend. The same is true about weddings. One of the things I have learned in working as a designer for over thirty years is that couples often have an easier time discussing money with a perfect stranger than they do with each other. So this is a good time for you and your soon-to-be husband to get comfortable with the subject.

> ## A frank discussion of budget is essential to the planning process.

If you come from a family that has difficulty speaking frankly about money, then your challenge will be even greater, especially if your parents are paying for the wedding. In fact, if your parents are paying, then there are considerations that you should make for their sake and yours—both financial and otherwise. The "otherwise" is the guest list and costs in general. Your parents may have guests whom they insist on inviting that you would probably not invite. If they are paying for your wedding, their guest list is something that you will have to find a way to negotiate. If you are paying and feel you cannot afford the extra guests, start compromising by simply acknowledging your parents' needs. As you refine your list of guests, let your parents participate. As they see the budget developing, ask for their input in making it balance, reserving your right to make final decisions. That way, they will know that you have tried to be considerate and they will respect and appreciate your efforts.

WEDDING COSTS CAN BE SHARED

Traditionally speaking, the bride's parents do pay for most of the wedding. But frankly speaking, things are changing. With the average wedding costing nearly twenty-seven thousand dollars (according to CNNMoney), more couples are either footing the bill themselves or at least contributing a good sum. In some instances, the groom's parents are taking on more responsibility as well. Occasionally, another relative or family friend may even choose to help out financially. When my niece got engaged, I told them I would pay for her wedding. I knew that my niece and her fiancé really wanted to start a family early and also that I would much rather see them use their savings as a down payment on a home than splurge on a big wedding. We agreed that I would give them just so much to spend. If they chose to spend more, it would have to come from their savings. They had a very nice wedding that accomplished everyone's goals and they bought a home within their first year of marriage. Ultimately, your objective should be to achieve and implement your dreams on a realistic budget.

When planning your budget, start by taking into consideration the "musts" from your list, your fiancé's list and lists from both sets of parents. It's important to understand that you cannot make everyone's dreams come true. You will need to pick and choose those things that will have the greatest impact, not only on your wedding but on your families as well. This will be hard. The best advice I can give you is to seek God's help and blessing on your decisions.

Putting together a budget can seem overwhelming, but don't get flustered. Using the list below, you can begin to make phone calls to potential reception locations, caterers, bridal shops, photographers, etc., to start plugging in numbers.

➤ Ceremony expenses (church or other location, pastor or other officiator, marriage license)
➤ Transportation
➤ Rings
➤ Prewedding parties and rehearsal dinner
➤ Reception, cake and food
➤ Florist
➤ Photographer
➤ Invitations
➤ Attire (bride's dress, veil, accessories, groom's outfit)

- ➤ Gifts for bridesmaids and groomsmen
- ➤ Accommodations for out-of-town attendants
- ➤ Honeymoon

Just glancing at this list, you can see how easy it would be to spend a fortune. TheKnot.com says, "It's easy to sink ten thousand dollars into a wedding. It's an art to do it for two thousand dollars." If you already know how much money you have to spend, as my niece did, then you can simply begin to divvy it up among the above categories and then adjust as you make your ultimate decisions on specific items. The only complaint heard at my niece's wedding was that the reception hall was too small for the amount of people. It was. Nonetheless, it was a very fun time.

The goal is to create a memory that you will cherish the rest of your life. Your wedding legacy should not be a huge debt and family strife. Be sure you are comfortable with the decisions you make and that those paying for it are comfortable too.

SIMPLICITY MADE SIMPLE

TRACK YOUR EXPENSES. You will be expected to make down payments for your rings, clothing, the reception hall, the cake and many other items. Keep track of these items as well as those things you purchase along the way. It's amazing how quickly several small, seemingly insignificant purchases can eat up a big portion of your budget. I recommend that you open a separate "wedding" checking account to make tracking your expenses easier.

TAKE INTO SERIOUS CONSIDERATION WHAT IS MORE IMPORTANT: a fancy wedding or a lavish honeymoon. Most of us cannot afford both. Perhaps a backyard reception is the answer to getting your dream honeymoon. Or you can do what a friend of mine did and postpone your honeymoon by several months or even a year. She was married in January but her honeymoon was in June. If, like my niece, you hope to purchase a home soon after being married, then this priority should be a major consideration in planning how much to spend on your wedding.

CONSIDER AN "OUT-OF-SEASON" WEDDING to save money. About seventy percent of weddings take place between May and October. If you schedule off-season, you should get a better deal on almost everything, from flowers to limousines. But be sure to avoid planning your wedding on a holiday. Most caterers, bands, etc., are booked a year or two in advance for holidays.

Don't be afraid to **LET YOUR FAMILY AND FRIENDS HELP**. I have helped two friends plan their weddings. One was married at a bed-and-breakfast on the beach and the entire wedding party slept there too. Our dresses were all bought "off the rack" to keep costs down. They were simple but beautiful and absolutely the perfect style for this lovely bride. We planned the whole wedding in two months. Think about the skills your friends have that could greatly contribute to your plans. I am kiddingly known for having the "gift of bossiness," which translates into being good at delegation.

The reception can eat up to fifty percent of your budget. Be selective when deciding among the options of a sit-down dinner, a buffet or simply hot hors d'oeuvres. Don't forget to discuss the cost of such things as tipping, insurance, service and overtime when meeting with caterers. Many offer "package" deals that usually cost less than choosing items à la carte. You may want to **CONSIDER A COMBINATION À LA CARTE/PACKAGE**. That's what I did. We only invited forty close friends and family to the dinner—but even that could have been very costly. We didn't give our guests a choice of meals—we chose chicken. We had a champagne toast and also offered to pay for one additional drink. If someone wanted more, then he or she had to pay for it. The caterer also provided our cake—that too helped to keep costs down. We provided our own music with exceptionally talented friends.

When it comes to photographers or videographers, don't take too many risks. This is **ONE AREA I WISH I HAD SPENT MORE MONEY ON.** Going cheap left us with hardly a good photo. (We'll get into greater detail on this later.)

DIVVY UP EXPENSES. If you are going with "traditional" rules, here is a list of who pays for what. The bride's family pays: *the entire cost of reception, rental of hall, caterer, wedding cake, beverages and gratuities* (the waiters, waitresses, bartenders and table captains should be tipped ten to fifteen percent, plus two to five percent for captains), *ceremony/reception flowers, bridesmaid bouquets, grandmothers' corsages, rice bags, ceremony/rental of sanctuary, fees for organist, soloist or choir, gratuities for policemen or other traffic control and transportation* (limousine driver should be tipped one to fifteen percent). The groom's family pays for the following: *their own traveling and hotel expenses, their own clothing and the rehearsal dinner and groom's cake.* The groom pays for: *wedding ring for bride, wedding gift for bride, groomsmen/usher gifts, clergymen/officiate fees, bride's bouquet, mothers' corsages, groom's boutonniere, ushers' boutonnieres and the marriage license.* The bride pays for: *wedding ring for groom, wedding gift for groom, bridesmaids' gifts, bridesmaids' luncheon, accommodations for out-of-town guests.*

> God, I ask that You direct us as we spend money on this event. Bless those who give financially to this event, and lead us to those who are gifted to oversee the responsibilities they assume. Amen.

Choosing Attendants and Guests

On the third day a wedding took place at Cana in Galilee.
Jesus' mother was there, and Jesus and his disciples had also
been invited to the wedding.

—JOHN 2:1–2 (NIV)

If it's any consolation, even having Jesus as a wedding guest will not guarantee a perfect wedding—the couple from Cana ran out of wine. Although you probably can't expect a guest to perform a miracle at your wedding, you should be able to count on a few good friends to make things run as smoothly as possible. That's why, when it comes to choosing your attendants, it's important to give serious thought to choosing at least one person you know you can always rely on. My friend Jan was my matron of honor, and she was such a big help. She escorted my out-of-town guests and family to and from their hotel to the church and the reception. She seemed to remember little details that if forgotten could have had a negative impact on the day—the kind of details that most brides cannot remember as the wedding day approaches.

The maid of honor or matron (if she is married) is usually the bride's sister, a cousin or her closest friend. She will be your personal attendant. It will be critical that you communicate your needs to her so she can be as helpful as possible. Your maid of honor's official duties include helping you shop for your gown, her gown and the bridesmaids' gowns. She should also lend a hand with all the tasks that will suddenly feel overwhelming for you to deal with. She will help with addressing invitations, putting together your favors, helping select flowers, the cake, etc. She will keep a record of all the gifts received. Of course, she and your bridesmaids will also throw your shower party.

> When choosing attendants, it's important to include at least one you know you can always rely on.

Rather than making a traditional shower, my friend Jan invited five of my closest friends to take me shopping at Victoria's Secret to buy me a wedding night negligee. It was so much fun—and a bit embarrassing. They would pick out an item for me to try and then I had to model it for them so they could all give their opinion. Afterward, we went to dinner at my favorite restaurant. It was the perfect party.

The day of the ceremony, your maid of honor will round up the bridesmaids and make sure they are ready to go on time. She will also keep the groom's ring safe during the ceremony. She will hold your bouquet while you exchange vows and rearrange your train as needed. She and the best man will also be the official witnesses and sign your marriage license. At your reception, they both will toast you and your new husband. She will dance with the best man during the official dance and make sure the other groomsmen get to dance as well. But the most important duty of your maid of honor is simply to keep you together emotionally. For me, Jan knew

Let your personality shine through in your table cards and consider tying them in to the theme of your wedding. Above are some examples of creative and interesting designs.

The formality of the reception is a key decision you will have to make: sit-down dinner or hors d'oeuvres; assigned seats or open tables; table settings; lighting . . . the list goes on . . . and on . . .

This floral chair drape adds a touch of elegance to the reception décor.

Church flowers can be quite expensive if not re-used at the reception.
Here, candles offer a simple and less costly alternative.

when to pray and when to busy herself with details and let me fuss. As you can see, the maid of honor is a very important person with a lot of responsibilities before and during the wedding.

My friend's daughter is getting married this summer. The bride wanted her best and oldest friend to officiate as her maid of honor. Sadly, that friend will be out of the country for several months prior to her wedding and will only arrive two weeks before. As a result, she won't be present to share the responsibilities that the maid of honor normally carries. If this young soon-to-be bride has someone else who is willing and able to help without the honor of being an attendant, or if the remaining bridesmaids will share the responsibilities, then perhaps things can still work out as the bride desires.

If you choose to have any bridesmaids in your wedding party, I caution you not to fall into the trap of only asking your friends. Decisions you make at this time can create potentially adverse repercussions. The best advice I can offer is to use great care and give much thought to your inclusion of family members as attendants. Family should be considered first. If you don't have a large family, then take this opportunity to create a sense of unity between your family and your groom's by asking one of his sisters to be a bridesmaid. This simple act will have long-lasting and positive benefits. The same goes for your groom; if you have a brother, then he should be asked to be an attendant as well.

> The most important duty of the maid of honor is to keep you together emotionally.

Bridesmaids also have official duties to perform. They will serve as auxiliary hostesses at your reception and introduce guests, instructing them to sign the guest book and to run last-minute errands, such as meeting with the florist and greeting the ceremony officiate. It's important to talk about this because it's easy to get distracted and simply have fun, forgetting what needs to be done. Your bridesmaids should also be willing to assist you with basic tasks such as accompanying you to the restroom to help with your gown and train.

GUESTS ARE AN IMPORTANT PART
OF YOUR PERFECT DAY

As we've discussed, the length of your guest list is going to greatly affect the cost of your wedding reception. Ultimately, if your parents are paying for the wedding, they are the ones who decide how many guests to include. If you and your groom are paying, then you decide how many guests and simply divide up that number evenly between your side and his—even if one of you has a larger family—unless the smaller family offers to do otherwise. I attended one wedding where the groom had a very small number of guests. I was thrilled to be asked if I wanted to be seated on his side of the church, even though I was a guest of the bride. Having a similar amount of guests on either side of the church made everyone feel more comfortable. And that, most of all, should be your goal—to make everyone comfortable.

Once you have determined how many guests you will have, you can choose the venue for your ceremony and reception. If you have chosen your location first, then it may, in fact, determine how many people can be accommodated. In the end, you will need to decide which is more important: the location or the number of guests.

I have a friend who is getting married this May. She wants a simple, inexpensive wedding. Yesterday, she said, "It has been anything but simple to plan." She is the youngest child and the only daughter. Her parents are up in years. They are very sweet, but they are rather set in their ways. Their wishes don't seem to be in line with their daughter's dream of a wedding. I know her parents, and I believe that they will eventually show consideration. I suggested that she stop the battle and just try to acknowledge the issues. Her parents love her, and I know they want the best for her. With the right approach on her part, they will respond to her heart's desires.

Some people seem to think that a wedding is an opportunity to invite every lost relative or friend from a lifetime. Or, perhaps you (or your fiancé) have friends that the other isn't exactly fond of. In this case, add a little grace along with the invitation and simply remember that you want to create warm memories, not battle wounds. Nonetheless, expect that there will be hurt feelings somewhere along the line. This is where temporary amnesia can really help. In keeping things simple, focus on what and who is important in the long run and make decisions accordingly.

One decision regarding guests that you need to make is whether or not to invite children. I suggest you consider your family's tradition on this. My family is large and there is always an abundance of little ones. As a result, we are all used to having them around. It just wouldn't be a celebration without their vibrant energy. This is your wedding day and everyone is there to honor your new life together. If the possibility of terrible-two tantrums happening in the middle of your vows is more stress than you can handle, then consider a child-free ceremony and let the little ones attend only the reception. If you choose this option, then please help locate babysitters for out-of-town guests with children. The same should be done if you have a child-free reception as well. The key is not to make any exceptions or you will surely cause hurt feelings—it's either no children or all children.

Another touchy area when it comes to guests is whether or not to allow single guests to bring a date. Most experts agree that unless the date is a "significant" other, i.e., a fiancé or a long-term relationship (five years or more together), then they should come alone. The more single friends you have, the more costly it can be to include a date for each one. On the other hand, it may be important to you to offer your single guests the option of bringing a companion.

SIMPLICITY MADE SIMPLE

When it comes to inviting guests, always include the spouse on the invitation for any married guest. Anyone participating in the wedding should also bring his or her spouse along. **BE CLEAR AND SPECIFIC WHEN ADDRESSING INVITATIONS.** For example, if you do not want children at your wedding, then simply address the invitation to Mr. and Mrs. Guest, and not The Guest Family, to avoid confusion. If someone RSVPs *with children* despite your efforts, it's okay to phone them and gently explain your preference.

BE SURE THAT ALL THE GROOM'S ATTENDANTS ARE AWARE OF THEIR DUTIES when asked to participate in your wedding. The best man has the most responsibility. He should help the groom select all the men's attire and follow up to be sure that all alterations are taken care of. He should also be sure that the entire order is complete. I cannot tell you how many times a cummerbund or a tie is missing. The best man will also be in charge of the marriage license, the bride's ring, airline tickets, the groom's wallet, keys and honeymoon hotel confirmation as well as being sure that the clergyman is paid. He will propose the first toast, dance with the bride and her mother and each of the bridesmaids. He will also be sure that your luggage is placed into your car for your honeymoon getaway.

IF YOU ARE INVITING CHILDREN, then consider setting up a children's area at the reception. You may even want to hire someone to entertain the little ones as well. If you choose not to invite children, make certain that all close friends and relatives are aware of your "no children policy" well in advance.

The number of ushers is directly related to the number of guests that need to be seated. I suggest assigning a head usher who can oversee the others. All should be well rehearsed in **THE FINE ART OF USHERING.** An usher should offer his right arm and walk women to their seats. The husband or escort can follow behind. If there is more than one woman in a party, the usher will offer his arm to the eldest and the others may follow behind. As he reaches the pew, he should turn to stand in front of the pew, facing the woman as she enters the pew. Once she is seated, he should offer her a wedding program. If he is seating a woman on the left side of the church, then it is appropriate for her to walk across in front of the usher, while he makes a counterclockwise move to stand in front of the pew. If all this sounds confusing, don't worry. Most churches and other places of worship have someone trained in this art who will help direct all of you. The ushers will also be responsible for lighting the candles at the designated time and extinguishing them at the end of the ceremony. Ushers should pay careful attention to the candles during the ceremony to be sure there are no surprises. They are also responsible for laying the aisle runner and removing it later.

Lord, thank You for giving us good friends
with whom to share this important day.
Please protect them as they travel to celebrate
with us, and help them to understand how their
joy is an important part of our own. Amen.

A Timeline Planner

I dreamed of a wedding of elaborate elegance;

a church filled with flowers and friends.

I asked him what kind of wedding he wished for;

he said one that would make me his wife.

—AUTHOR UNKNOWN

I love the simple truth expressed in the quote above. So many of us dream of our wedding day from the time we are a child. We play "dress-up bride" over and over again and never tire of it. But the guys, well, let's just say we should be grateful that they are willing to play along with our little fantasy. To be fair, there are plenty of guys who do enjoy taking part in some of the planning. And many of them love planning romantic surprises. But for the most part, the bulk of the planning and organizing will be up to the women. If you are not the organized type, then I suggest you enlist the help of your most organized friend or relative. Organization is critical to making your dreams come true.

The first thing you will need to decide on is a wedding date. According to experts, the ideal length of time to plan a formal wedding is twelve months. However, many beautiful weddings have been planned in far less time. In fact, sometimes having less time can make the entire planning process easier because you simply have to make decisions more quickly. You can purchase a wedding planner/workbook/guide or go online and download one. *Brides Magazine* provides a free twelve-month countdown online at www.brides.com.

> Once you have established a date, create a timeline countdown calendar.

Many bridal magazines also include personal planning guides in special issues. Once you have established a date you can create a timeline countdown calendar. But before you start marking your calendar, make an appointment with your minister or other religious leader to discuss the date and time for the ceremony. Most churches book weddings far in advance. Unless there is a very specific reason for your choice of date, remain reasonably flexible and don't get your heart too determined. From experience, I can tell you the date really doesn't make that big a difference in the long run. It's your intentions that matter.

The next decision you have to make is whether or not to use a professional wedding planner. A friend of mine chose to use a planner because she only had three months to plan her wedding. The expert took off the pressure and made the entire process easier. The wedding planner already had a knowledge base of caterers, florists, printers, etc., on instant recall. She knew which questions to ask and how to get things done efficiently and within budget. Some brides hire a professional right from the beginning and others simply hire a coordinator for the last week of preparations. You may also choose to enlist the help of someone you know who has planned other weddings successfully.

If you are choosing to have a "destination" wedding, then I think it's essential to have a wedding planner/coordinator. A destination wedding is one that takes place at the honeymoon location. I have just been invited to a Las Vegas destination wedding. At first, I was skeptical, but after talking with the bride and checking out the Web site for the Venetian Resort in Las Vegas, I must admit, I am very impressed. My friend chose Las Vegas because she wanted to keep things simple and inexpensive. You can have a wedding there starting from $1,250. The wedding includes a custom bouquet and matching groom's boutonniere, a video of the ceremony, thirty-minute rehearsal and a champagne toast gift set. The wedding takes place in a small romantic chapel that can hold approximately forty people. Their on-staff coordinator handles everything for you.

BREATHE DEEPLY

Now, take a deep breath and release it slowly. Repeat. This is a little exercise I want you to practice every time you begin to feel overwhelmed. You will be required to make so many decisions that you may feel inundated with pressure. Practice relaxation techniques and simply focus on one step at a time. Here are the basics you need to cover over the next several months:

As Soon as Possible:
➤ Meet with your clergyperson to set a date and arrange for premarital counseling.
➤ Set a budget and determine the style of wedding you prefer. Decide on the ceremony and reception locations.

Eight to Twelve Months Before:
➤ Interview and confirm agreements with photographers, florists, bakers and caterers.

- ➤ Choose attendants.
- ➤ Purchase your gown and your attendants' gowns.
- ➤ Send your "Save the Date" cards.
- ➤ Send your engagement announcement to a local newspaper.
- ➤ Put together your guest list.

Four to Six Months Before:
- ➤ Register for gifts.
- ➤ Research and book your honeymoon. Apply for passports if needed.
- ➤ Order wedding invitations and thank-you notes.
- ➤ Purchase wedding rings.
- ➤ Reserve the groom's (and his attendants') attire.
- ➤ Choose favors.
- ➤ Make your wedding night hotel reservations.

Two to Four Months Before:
- ➤ Plan your ceremony. Visit with your clergy or church coordinator to go over your vows, readings and music.
- ➤ Shop for your honeymoon lingerie and clothing.
- ➤ Mail your invitations.
- ➤ Schedule rehearsal time and dinner.
- ➤ Choose gifts for your attendants.
- ➤ Arrange transportation for the day of the wedding.
- ➤ Send change-of-address forms to the post office.
- ➤ Make reservations for out-of-town guests.

Six Weeks Before:
- ➤ Have a final fitting of your dress.
- ➤ Get your programs printed.

- ➤ Make two appointments for hair and makeup; make one at least a week in advance in order to "try on" your wedding hairdo before the big day.
- ➤ Purchase a guest book.
- ➤ Get your blood tests and obtain marriage license.
- ➤ Get a physical and any inoculations necessary for travel.
- ➤ Contact newspaper(s) about wedding announcement.

Two Weeks Before:
- ➤ Make a seating plan and write place cards.
- ➤ Notify the caterer of final guest count.
- ➤ Break in your wedding shoes—scuff up the soles so you don't "skate" down the aisle.
- ➤ Pick up your dress.
- ➤ Give specific responsibilities to each of your attendants.
- ➤ Confirm honeymoon reservations.
- ➤ Have your teeth cleaned/whitened.

One Week Before:
- ➤ Pack for your wedding night and honeymoon.
- ➤ Confirm details with the caterer.
- ➤ Finalize the seating plan.
- ➤ Meet with the church coordinator for a walk-through rehearsal.

One Day Before:
- ➤ Have a manicure and pedicure and a bikini waxing, if you dare.
- ➤ Prepare tip and payment envelopes and assign someone to distribute them.

➤ It may not be possible to invite everyone to your wedding, and some friends and family may live too far away to attend. Prepare marriage announcements and give them to an attendant to mail after the wedding.

Your Wedding Day:
➤ Praise God and enjoy!

SIMPLICITY MADE SIMPLE

Enjoy your wedding countdown with **SPIRITUAL GUIDANCE** from God's Word. Consider doing a study of the Song of Solomon with your groom. Tommy Nelson, a pastor and popular conference teacher, has a wonderful Bible study series on God's best for love, marriage, sex and romance. He also holds weekend-long conferences on the subject. Consider locating one near you and signing up. It will be well worth it. Or you may want to study the Psalms—simply read one together each day.

To keep your fiancé on schedule, **CREATE A COUNTDOWN CALENDAR FOR YOUR GROOM.** Here are a few ideas you can suggest: He can help with the guest list and making arrangements to meet with your pastor or religious leader of choice. He can: assist with the gift registry; make medical/dental appointments six weeks in advance; shop for wedding rings; select the best man and ushers; order his and his attendants' wedding attire; shop for a house/apartment; work on ceremony plans; arrange transportation; have duplicate keys made for each of you. My sweetie took charge of creating and printing our invitations and wedding programs on his computer. I really appreciated his effort. He also was a big help in selecting music for our ceremony. But the most important thing he did was simply to arrive on time for our wedding.

CHOOSE YOUR WEDDING PLANNER/CONSULTANT WITH CARE. A diverse variety of people claim to be professionals. For example, salesclerks at major bridal salons or department stores are often available as wedding planners. They work on commission, which makes me a bit skeptical. After all, the less you want to spend, the less they earn, which might make their attention span a little short too. If you want a trained, full-time professional, then contact a member of the Association of Bridal Consultants. A wedding planner is someone who assists the bride throughout her planning process. Planners will help contact vendors, meet with you to check out locations and help choose colors and design ideas. A wedding director is someone who assists you and your family on the day of the wedding. Directors usually arrive one hour prior to the ceremony. They will make sure that everyone has flowers and boutonnieres. They will literally direct the wedding party down the aisle and into their places at the altar. The wedding director will stay with you throughout the ceremony and assist at the reception. Some wedding planners also work as directors.

PLAN AHEAD FOR A DESTINATION WEDDING. If you plan on bringing your gown with you, carry it on the plane in a hanging bag. Then make arrangements to have any wrinkles steamed out when you arrive at your destination. Island and cruise weddings are very popular. Most islands and cruise lines offer complete packages and are equipped to pull together the entire affair easily. Key things to consider when choosing a destination wedding are the laws of the region and necessary documentation. For example, you can be married in the Cayman Islands in one day. Other islands require a three- to four-day wait. You will also want to consider weather. The Caribbean in hurricane season or Colorado in the winter can be tricky. If you are inviting guests, know the travel costs so you can inform them before they accept your invitation. You may be able to get a group rate, so guests can save some money. Alert any guests of your destination plans as far in advance as you can. Most will need to schedule vacation time to accommodate such a trip.

Lord, I choose to fully rest in the knowledge
that all things will work together
beautifully because You are our ultimate
wedding planner and director. Amen.

A Symbol of Your Love

Behold, thou *art* fair, my love;

behold, thou *art* fair;

thou *hast* doves' eyes. . . .

—SONG OF SOLOMON 4:1 (KJV)

Reading this verse can make one feel awkward because it is such an intensely private and intimate exchange between two lovers. But the passionate feelings of love and admiration expressed are universal to couples in love. A ring is also a universal symbol of love, and although there is no specific biblical origin attached to an engagement ring, it is a time-honored tradition of public declaration of your promised betrothal and upcoming marriage. The exchanging of rings has also become an essential part of most wedding ceremonies.

When diamonds were first discovered in India around 800 BC, they were prized for their rarity and beauty throughout the world. Some people even believed that diamonds possessed magical powers. Gemologists, jewelers and buyers were also impressed with the hardness of the diamond. The name diamond comes from the

Greek word *adamas*, which means "unconquerable," thus making the diamond the perfect choice to represent the unique bond of marriage.

Popular ring styles obviously have varied over time. Victorian era rings (1835–1900) were often set in yellow or rose gold. Some were simple and others were more elegant and intricate in design. Many of the Victorian settings featured rows of diamonds, cut with extra facets on the bottom. They often included pearls as well. The classic Tiffany six-pronged diamond solitaire was first introduced in 1886. In the Edwardian era (1900–1920), platinum engagement rings were first introduced. Jewelers began crafting incredibly detailed styles with pierced shapes, scrollwork and filigree on the mountings. I must admit that I love the craftsmanship of an Edwardian-style ring. Jewelers also began to use stones other than diamonds. Rose-cut stones and brilliant sapphires became very popular during this time. And the art deco period (1920–1930) brought out the jazzy, artistic and streamlined geometric-style rings. Egyptian, Asian and Native American cultures also influenced this period and the style of the rings greatly.

> A ring is a universal symbol of love and an essential part of most wedding ceremonies.

Today, brides-to-be opt for the classic single, round diamond solitaire most often. And many brides are choosing a platinum setting because it not only makes the diamond look more brilliant, but it is also stronger and more valuable than gold. Ultimately, you should choose a ring because you love it and not because it seems trendy or fashionable—or even valuable.

When it comes to finding your ring, take your time and do a lot of browsing before making a decision. Today some folks are choosing to shop on the Internet, but I don't recommend this, at least not initially. You really need to try on rings. My husband had promised me a tenth anniversary ring. As I began browsing, I discovered that most rings were simply too large in overall proportion for my hand. In the end, I found a ring I loved that the original designer agreed to recast a third smaller to accommodate my finger.

There are four *C*s that are important when choosing a diamond. First, the *cut*: This is the term that refers to the shape of the stone. The classic *round* stone has fifty-seven or fifty-eight facets, which make it sparkle. The *heart-*, *oval-* and *pear-*shaped stones resemble their names. The *pear*-shaped cut should be worn with the point facing away from your body to make your finger look longer. The *marquise* cut is similar to oval with pointed ends on either side. The *princess* cut is a brilliant square-shaped stone. The *emerald* cut was originally designed specifically for emeralds and is rectangular with cropped corners and stair-steplike facets cut into it. The *asscher* is similar to the emerald cut, but square rather than rectangular. And the *cushion* cut is a cross between an oval and a rectangular-style cut.

The second *C* is *clarity*. The fewer internal flaws (or inclusions) rings have, the more valuable they are. Most of these flaws can be seen only with a microscope and include light and dark spots, tiny cracks, blemishes, pits, scratches and nicks. The fewer inclusions in a diamond, the more rare and valuable it is.

The third *C* stands for *carat*. This is the weight of the diamond. It can be difficult to determine carat size simply by comparing the physical size because the same weight of diamond can appear larger or smaller depending on how it is cut. For example, oval-, marquise- and pear-shaped stones can often seem bigger than a round cut.

The fourth *C* is *color*. Diamond color is rated on a scale from *D*, which is virtually colorless and the most valuable, to *Z*, which has traces of yellow or brown. There

> The four *C*s are important to consider when choosing a diamond.

are also naturally colored stones that are becoming more popular. Naturally colored diamonds are known as "fancies" and can come in such hues as pink, yellow and blue. These are extremely rare and therefore the most expensive diamonds. Because they are so rare, they are not even graded on the *D–Z* scale. The more saturated the color, the more expensive they are.

CHOOSING PRECIOUS METALS

Once you have chosen your diamond shape and color, you need to choose your precious metal. Start with color: yellow or white. Gold is measured in carats according to its percent of purity, with twenty-four carat being 99.99 percent pure gold. Twelve carat (12k) gold is composed of fifty percent real gold and fifty percent alloy. Fourteen carat (14k) is a good choice because it is strong, holds its shape well, and it will shine brilliantly for years. Eighteen carat (18k) gold is seventy-four percent real gold. It's more expensive but it is also softer and therefore less durable.

If you prefer a white metal then you have two choices: platinum or white gold. White gold is made by blending pure gold with alloy and nickel. Nickel is what gives gold the white color orientation. White gold is a great choice if you like the look of platinum but can't afford it, because white gold is one-third the cost of platinum. It's also a good choice for a smaller/detailed ring because it is more malleable than platinum. However, be aware that over time, white gold turns a faint yellow or off-white shade.

Platinum is ninety-five percent pure platinum and five percent iridium or palladium. Platinum is considered the ultimate precious metal for rings. In the course of time, however, it too will change slightly in appearance, eventually taking on a beautiful brushed, antique patina. This is considered a sign of quality.

Whatever your style choice in rings, the key is simply to communicate this information to your betrothed. Some gals (like me) like to shop for their own ring. Others like to be surprised. But no one wants a disappointing surprise.

My family had a close call when my brother announced he was getting engaged. Mom was so excited about the possibility of giving my brother a treasured family heirloom ring set. Fortunately, Mom spoke to me about this before she proceeded with this gift idea. It was also fortunate that my brother chose to speak to me about the experience he had shopping for the engagement ring with his fiancé. She had very clear and specific ideas about the kind of ring she wanted to wear for a lifetime. And the family heirloom did not figure in. I was able to break the news to Mom gently before she spent any money having the antique rings cleaned and restored.

SIMPLICITY MADE SIMPLE

BE TRUE TO YOURSELF AND YOUR LIFESTYLE. Be sure that the ring you choose will still make you smile twenty years from now. I knew that my work as a designer would be very rough on most settings. I wanted something simple but elegant. My choice was a diamond eternity ring that doubles as my engagement and wedding ring all in one. Remember that you will wear this ring every day. Choose something that can seamlessly become a part of your life.

CONSIDER A TWO-TONED COLOR METAL. By combining both gold and white precious metals you will easily complement any other jewelry you wear, whether it's silver or gold. However, never mix a platinum engagement ring with a white gold band because the different metals will rub against each other and over time will start to wear each other out. If you are allergic to most metals, then platinum is your best bet. It is the least likely metal to cause an allergic reaction.

SET A BUDGET. You and your fiancé need to agree on how much you are going to invest in rings. Once you have agreed—don't tempt yourself by looking at rings that exceed your budget—you will only set yourself up for disappointment.

DECIDE WHAT MATTERS MOST—size or clarity. A friend of mine has a very large diamond engagement ring. But it suits her perfectly. It is exactly the kind of ring we all expected her to choose. Another friend chose a nearly flawless tiny single solitaire stone. Beauty is in the eye of the beholder.

FIND THE "RIGHT" SIZE. That may sound like a simple suggestion but it is not. Remember you will wear your rings for a lifetime and that may include pregnancies, menstruation, and while exercising and throughout all seasons. Have your ring sized when you are calm and your body temperature is at normal. Never finalize your size in the morning because women tend to retain salt from the day before. Also, don't have your ring sized after you've just exercised (fingers swell) or when you are extremely hot or cold.

CONSIDER ENGRAVING THE INSIDE OF YOUR RINGS. It not only makes them more personal but also serves as a "birthmark" should you ever lose it. Most jewelers can do it for you. Prices start at a dollar per character (for a simple font) and go up to seven dollars per character for more elaborate fonts.

Don't forget to insure your ring. You will need a detailed description with value included to present to your insurance agent. Also remember that **THE GREATEST RISK FOR LOSING A RING OCCURS WHILE YOU ARE TRAVELING.** Wear your ring at all times when you are away from home; avoid removing your rings to wash your hands, etc. I do remove mine because I have eczema, so I take my rings off every night. When I travel, I pack a jewelry case and am sure to always place my jewelry and rings inside it as soon as I remove them to keep from forgetting them.

THINK ABOUT WHETHER OR NOT YOU WANT A "RING BEARER" TO CARRY YOUR REAL RINGS DOWN the aisle. Most couples choose to have plastic rings attached to the pillow rather than risk the loss and accompanying stress if the real rings take a fall. Ring bearers are usually four to ten years old and are dressed for the occasion in attire to complement the flower girl's dress or in a tiny tuxedo. If you choose to include a ring bearer in your ceremony, be sure to assign a bridesmaid or usher to keeping this little one in line, on time and contentedly busy.

> Lord, I am grateful that Your love for us
> is without beginning or end, just like
> the circle of the rings we exchange. Help us
> to understand Your unconditional love as we
> embrace endless love for each other. Amen.

PART THREE

A Day for Adornment

As a bride, **THIS IS YOUR DAY TO ADORN YOURSELF** in a dress that makes you feel like the royal princess you are in spirit. Choosing a dress is easy if you remain true to yourself—simply select the dress that expresses your unique God-given style. Beautiful wedding dresses are available in all prices, so I have included advice in this section from an expert gown designer to explain the differences of selections. As with the gown, the music and the flowers you choose should be what *you* enjoy—so follow your own instincts. I will share tips for choosing a photographer and even registering for wedding gifts so that you and your groom can derive the most pleasure from the parties that will be held in your honor.

Your dress will become a lasting symbol of your wedding and the focal point of many photos. Choose one you think you will still adore ten years from now.

When choosing a bridal bouquet, you can go very simple, with a few of your favorite blooms . . .

or more traditional, with a full bouquet of mixed flowers.

As important as selecting your dress is selecting a seamstress who is experienced in wedding gown alterations.

Children can bring a special joy to your wedding celebration. But know the child—
some little ones may be uncomfortable with all of the attention.

Dressing the Part

All glorious is the princess within her chamber;

her gown is interwoven with gold.

In embroidered garments she is led to the king. . . .

—PSALM 45:13–14 (NIV)

Psalm forty-five is titled "A wedding song," obviously written for the royal couple. The beautiful bride is adorned in a magnificent gown made of gold-embroidered fabric. Embroidery on clothing, which involves detailed needlework by skilled craftsmen, was as highly valued then as it is today. But embroidery is just one of the many details you may choose for your wedding gown. Choosing your gown can be one of the most stressful parts of your wedding planning. It can be your personal signature— a reflection of who you are now and who you hope to become in the future. For this moment, it is a statement of your very identity!

To help you choose the most perfect wedding gown, I went to one of the top wedding dress designers, Janell Berté. Berté has designed spectacular gowns for her high-profile clients, such as Jill Ireland, Fay Wray and Zsa Zsa Gabor. Many of her designs can be viewed on her Web site at www.berte.com. Most recently, her bridal designs caught the eye of Hollywood when she was asked to make twenty-four gowns for the film *Something New*, starring Sanaa Lathan. I was able to sit with this amazing designer simply because her company is located here in little Lancaster, Pennsylvania. Berté is a remarkable, down-to-earth woman. And although her clientele list includes celebrity names, the majority of them are ordinary women in their late twenties and early thirties.

Berté says it is most important for you to choose a gown for "you," and not to be influenced by all your friends. She believes that too often young women bring their group of good friends and family to help choose a dress. It is difficult when you have several opinions to know which one to listen to. You simply don't need five or six opinions. Berté suggests bringing along only one or two people who can distinguish between their own tastes and yours—and articulate the difference. She also believes that bridal gown professionals should be trusted to suggest a dress that is appropriate for your body shape and size.

> When choosing your gown, think about how you will feel looking at your wedding photos ten years from now.

Berté said that one of the problems today is that Hollywood is setting the trends. She warns that just because these highly successful young actresses have tons of money to spend, it doesn't mean they show good taste. In fact, the problem is compounded by the fact that Hollywood, it seems to me, has no rules, etiquette or respect for tradition. Following any example of this ilk, in my opinion, is not a good idea.

Berté suggests thinking about how you will feel looking at your wedding photos ten years from now. Today, women are aspiring to professional careers more than ever before. You will want to display your wedding photo on your desk proudly and not be embarrassed. Because about one-third of couples are now paying for or contributing to their own wedding, Berté suggests spending a little bit more on the dress so you have a long-lasting impression that will make you proud later. Perhaps that is why Berté's gowns are so classic in style.

TRUST YOUR OWN INSTINCTS

The practical side of Berté reminds us that this one dress is simply for *your* wedding ceremony. It is doubtful that your daughter or granddaughter will want to or be able to wear your gown. In most cases, thinking otherwise is merely a romantic fantasy. Statistics say that only one-tenth of a percent of gowns are ever worn by another generation.

Most designers have both a high-priced and lower-priced line of gowns. Berté has two lines of wedding dresses that range in price from a high of $6,000 down to $1,500. What makes the difference? The less expensive gowns are manufactured overseas—usually in China—and are not one of a kind. The couture line is made here in Lancaster, Pennsylvania, and is designed specifically for the individual bride. Obviously, your choice of fabrics also affects prices. Today, most of the beaded fabrics come from India, where workers hand-apply the beads to yards and yards of fabric. A couture wedding gown bodice that is beaded, for example, will be sewn from such fabric. In addition, the seamstress will use beads from leftover fabric and hand-sew them over seams to camouflage them. This is a time-consuming and costly process that will influence the price of the gown.

Of course, a gown made of silk rather than polyester will be more costly. That will not make it more resilient, however. Silk is a fragile fabric. Polyester is basically

> Choose a gown that reflects your style— not the opinions of others.

plastic—and, therefore, nearly indestructible. If you know that you want to keep your gown and are a tomboy at heart—purchase a polyester gown and enjoy worry-free fun.

SIMPLICITY MADE SIMPLE

After your wedding, it's time to **STORE YOUR GOWN**. Berté does not believe in having a gown dry-cleaned. The chemicals used in dry cleaning begin to break down fabric and change its color. Silk will change color regardless of whether or not you dry-clean it. Berté recommends simply having the dry cleaner spot clean the hem of your gown and any other spots you may have detected. However, there is one association of dry cleaners that professionals like Berté use; they can be located at www .americasbestcleaners.com. The cost is around five hundred dollars per dress. Berté said she would not consider this unless your gown is in the five thousand dollar range. It simply doesn't make sense. She suggests storing your gown in a box approximately 28 x 17 x 6 inches. Place a clean white sheet in the box. Then fold your gown in half and place it gently on the sheet. Fold the sheet over the gown, close the box and store it in a dry, cool "living" place. In other words, a room in your home that is air-conditioned and where the temperature is between fifty and seventy-five degrees.

For a "destination wedding," Berté says there are two ways to **TRANSPORT YOUR GOWN**. One is to ship it via UPS or FedEx—insured. However, she recommends hand-carrying it after double bagging it carefully. Start with a Pellon bag, which is usually available through your wedding dress supplier. Then place it in a plastic garment bag because you absolutely do NOT want your gown to get wet. Once wet, it is ruined. Berté said most destination locations are prepared to steam your gown upon arrival. But you can also press your gown using a pressing cloth and a steam iron. If your gown is beaded, carefully press it on the back side, not the outside.

Once you have taken possession of your gown, it is your responsibility. **IF YOU ARE PLANNING ON HAVING PHOTOS TAKEN** in any location where your gown may get soiled—wait until after the ceremony. You do not want to walk down the aisle with a dirty hem. Berté says beachside wedding photos really can be harmful to a wedding gown. The damp salt air may leave your gown limp. Again, she cautions that you wait until after the ceremony to have your photos taken.

Choose a gown that makes sense for you and your body type. It starts with proportion. Nancy Aucone of the Wedding Salon of Manhasset on Long Island in New York, says, "The dress may be gorgeous, but you will never look right if the lines are wrong. **THINK OF YOUR SILHOUETTE.** Begin with your best features, then ease into the ones that are less than perfect. Do you have a tiny waist? Great cleavage? A lovely swan neck? Wonderful shoulders? Show them off!" If you are petite, then a straight sheath style can be the perfect choice. It's long and fitted close to the body, which elongates your profile. If you prefer a more traditional style, then choose an A-line or princess silhouette that is fitted on the top and widens to a cone shape—it's more streamlined and won't overwhelm you. A bateau neck style is an excellent choice if you have pretty shoulders. If not, then a sleeveless scoop bodice will nicely accent slender arms. Check out the Web site at www.weddingchannel.com for a guide that helps you determine whether you are a Classic, Natural, Hip, Romantic, Fashion Plate or Diva style bride.

Start early and **TAKE YOUR TIME** when shopping for a bridal gown. Consult professionals if you're not sure which kind of dress is right for you. They can help you choose the right cut, fabric, size and price. The most important thing is that your dress makes you feel beautiful and confident. WeddingChannel suggests filtering out the emotional baggage that might cause you to make a bad choice. Don't let your childhood fantasy of a swirling, sumptuous ball gown (bejeweled to the max) be in charge of this decision. You are a grown woman. Be realistic and practical; allow your gown to accent your best features and play down the rest.

MAKE SURE THE DRESS FITS. Most wedding gowns require at least two fittings to get it right. If you are having a custom gown made, then expect several fittings. Most department store and bridal salons offer alterations. Make sure that they take full responsibility for any alterations they do. If you choose to have an outside seamstress do your alterations—be careful. You can find someone who is qualified but you must do your homework and check references. Make sure that wedding gowns are a specialty and not something done only occasionally. Word of mouth is always the best source for locating any professional. Your bridal shop may also recommend someone. Firmly communicate a clear deadline. Also, avoid last-minute stress by having your dress alterations finished at least four weeks in advance.

DON'T FORGET THE NECESSITIES FOR *UNDER* YOUR GOWN. Lacy, beautiful lingerie should be part of your wedding ensemble. This is another area where a professional with expert advice can make a big difference. For a strapless gown, a bustier or merry widow is the most popular choice. The boning and construction of a bustier provides better support than a simple strapless bra. The snug fit also ensures that you have a smooth waistline. For a sheath style gown, you want to avoid boning, lace, ribbons or other details that might poke through, creating ugly bumps under your dress. Look instead for a seamless bodysuit, preferably thong-style. Microfiber is the smoothest of fabrics and provides a perfect silhouette. A sleeveless gown usually has straps wide enough that you can wear most lingerie. A body-slimming bones bustier with straps is one good option. But do consider the fabric of your dress; thinner, more delicate fabric might show through the lace or other appliqué details of your bustier. A good choice again would be microfiber. A backless gown is dramatic, but it also can be problematic when it comes to finding just the right underpretties. An adhesive bra is one choice that can work well. Just be sure that it includes underwire for support and has large adhesive tapes that will hold for up to twelve hours. If you are a well-endowed bride, the experts suggest taping a "U" shape around your breast, making sure the tape covers the entire bottom half of the cup.

> Lord, thank You for giving me the status
> of a princess in my inheritance through Christ.
> As I dress to become a bride, cover me
> in Your love and bless me to become
> a godly wife to this man whom I love. Amen.

Music and Flowers

David told the leaders of the Levites to appoint

their brothers as singers

to sing joyful songs, accompanied by musical instruments:

lyres, harps and cymbals.

—1 CHRONICLES 15:16 (NIV)

The role of music in our lives is attested to simply by the many pictures of instruments found in ancient Egyptian ruins. From ancient Egypt to today—music has permeated our daily lives. We use music to celebrate, mourn and even create better working atmospheres. Music stirs our souls and calms our minds. It is powerful. So don't take choosing music for your wedding lightly! The overall mood and atmosphere of the wedding ceremony and reception will be affected by your selection of music.

By now, you know that I want your wedding to be "your way." However, I must warn you that simply choosing music that you love, particularly at the reception, can backfire. I read about one young couple who loved jazz. They chose to have unremitting jazz for their entire reception. Sadly, there were very few jazz lovers attending. Most folks either left early or simply gathered among themselves and ignored the music. You will enjoy the reception more if you sense that everyone is having a good time. The easiest way to accomplish this is to mix up the music to range from traditional waltzes to contemporary styles that younger folks will enjoy. If you want to incorporate an ethnic flair to your wedding, music is one of the best ways to achieve this.

> The overall mood and atmosphere of the wedding ceremony and reception will be affected by your selection of music.

The first decision you have to make is whether to use live music or a DJ. A DJ will almost always be less expensive, but that doesn't mean live music is out of the question. I have seen many couples successfully incorporate both. Since most receptions last approximately four hours, choosing to have live music for the special dances (perhaps the second hour of the reception) and a DJ for the rest of the reception might be a nice compromise. Because music is so important, take your time and actually listen to prospective musicians in an environment that is similar to the one you expect your wedding to have. It is perfectly acceptable for you to attend weddings or other events at which they are playing. Obviously, you would not participate in the activities or have dinner, but you can stand to the side and listen to the band. Just be sure the musicians have cleared it first with those hosting the events. Another option that I recently discovered is a DJ who also happens to be a gifted vocalist. She brought prerecorded music with her—sort of like karaoke, but much better—and then simply sang with it. In addition, she also performed the role of a DJ and even helped orchestrate the evening by introducing the special dances, the bouquet throw, the cake cutting and other highlights.

Another option to consider is family and friends. But only do this if there are actually gifted musicians among them. I was fortunate because we had several musicians and vocalists as friends. That not only made it easy, but it also made it more meaningful because they knew Dave and me well and they felt honored to be asked. I've also heard of couples that have included the children's choir in their church as part of their ceremony music. String quartets, trumpets and even bagpipes can be played. That's what one friend of mine chose to do (he was obviously Scottish). The wedding party attire was based on a Scottish theme and the groom and groomsmen all wore traditional Scottish kilts. It was wonderful!

SURROUND YOURSELF WITH FLOWERS

Every bride should have a signature bouquet. It should be something special filled with sentiment, symbolism and dreams. Flowers create the visual backdrop and add an aromatic atmosphere to delight the senses. Some say it is the simplest way to remind us to take the time to (literally) smell the roses. And roses are still one of the most popular choices when it comes to bridal bouquets. But they are certainly not the only choice. In fact, there are so many options available that it would be hard to list them all here. If you have a favorite flower, that makes your choice simple.

David Stark, author of *To Have and To Hold: Magical Wedding Bouquets*, believes that using a single flower for your entire wedding can be charming and inspiring. He says daisies are a good example of how just one flower can advance an overall design theme. It is "spectacularly happy, indefatigably sunny, and it radiates innocence and country charm. Yet with the right treatment, it can be reimagined in an ultrasophisticated role." He even suggests that a flower girl scatter daisy heads rather than rose petals down the aisle. Best of all, daisies are very reasonably priced, making it possible to stretch your floral budget. Considering that the average cost of wedding flowers is now between eight hundred and one thousand dollars—that would be a very good idea.

Your flowers should reflect your style and your stature. For example, if you are tall, a cascading bouquet can be the perfect accessory to your ensemble. However, if you are not, like me, then a small bouquet makes more sense. Are you a classic bride? Then stick with a simple, sophisticated and timeless design for your bouquet. White roses or stephanotis are perfect. However, the stephanotis will need to have an extender inserted into them to work. A modern bride may choose to have something trendier. The single flower idea, as Stark suggested, or a monochromatic nosegay of calla lilies can be perfect. If choosing calla lilies, then you could use various shades for your attendants. If you dream of being the glamorous bride and making your own dramatic statement, then certainly let your flowers do the talking. Giant peonies or black magic roses have all the charisma you will need. You might even consider creating contrast in your bouquet by using circular rows of flowers in light and darker colors to create a bull's-eye effect. A romantic bride can be complemented with a simple small nosegay or tussy mussy (a cone-shaped vase) with roses, or even dahlias, surrounded by a cloud of baby's breath.

SIMPLICITY MADE SIMPLE

DON'T BE AFRAID TO ASK FOR HELP IN SELECTING YOUR MUSIC. Most churches have someone on staff, or can recommend someone who has plenty of experience. Planning/choreographing your wedding music is critical. For a traditional wedding, your overall plan should include music for the following sections of your program: *The Prelude, Processional, Ceremony* and *Recessional*. Often a vocalist or ensembles are used for the prelude. For your reception the areas for which to consider having music are: *cocktail hour, couple's first dance, bride and father's dance, groom and mother's dance, guests' first dance, dinner, dancing, cake cutting* and *last dance.*

BE PREPARED WHEN YOU MEET WITH THE FLORIST. Know how much you want to spend and bring a photo of your gown—showing several views—and swatches of fabric for your gown and your bridal party dresses as well. If you are not sure of the kind of flowers you prefer, be open to suggestions from the florist. When it comes to ribbons—be certain that they are using "natural" colors or "colorfast" dyed ribbons. The last thing you want is your dress ruined because the beautiful shade of green that you chose for the ribbon has bled into your beautiful white gown.

CONSIDER EACH ONE OF THE FOLLOWING AREAS WHEN CHOOSING FLOWERS. *Bride's flowers*: bouquet, headpiece (to be used either instead of a veil or later at the reception when you remove your veil) and throw-away bouquet; *bridesmaids' flowers*; *groom's boutonnieres* (or you could choose to simply use silk handkerchiefs instead); *flower girls and junior bridesmaids*; *ring bearer*; *mothers' corsages*; *grandmothers' corsages*; *church flowers*—chancel, aisles, windows, altar, candles and candelabras. You also need to consider flowers for your reception, such as table centerpieces for the bride's table, parents' table and guests' tables. Be sure that your centerpieces are either above eye level (by using tall narrow-stemmed vases) or no more than fourteen inches high, so that your guests can see each other across the table. You may want to consider using flowers for your *wedding cake decoration*—this can actually be less expensive than an ornately decorated cake. You may also add flowers to your buffet table, powder room and even the bride's and groom's chairs.

TRY SHARING FLOWERS. If there is a wedding immediately prior to or following yours at the same church, consider sharing the cost of church flowers. The other option is to simply reuse the church flowers at your reception. But discuss these options well in advance with your florist so that arrangements can be created that are adaptable. Choose "in-season" flowers to save on your budget.

To locate a florist, **START BY GETTING RECOMMENDATIONS** from friends, family and your church or other place of worship. You may want to consider making an appointment for a consultation. It might cost you a little (about thirty-five dollars an hour), but it will definitely be worth it. You want someone with whom you are totally comfortable. View their work, not only in photos, but in real life as well. Find out when their next wedding is scheduled and ask to see it. Be prepared to pose questions: Will they be willing to transport the flowers from your ceremony to the reception site? Will there be someone there to help assist you on the day of the wedding with pinning on boutonnieres and corsages? Will this cost extra? A boutonniere should be worn on the left side lapel. And pin it *under* the lapel so the pin doesn't show.

Thank You, Lord, for creating music and flowers
to fill our everyday lives with reason to celebrate.
Help us to keep the sweet harmony
and fragrance of our wedding day alive
throughout our marriage. Amen.

Photo Memories

There are always two people in every picture:
the photographer and the viewer.

—ANSEL ADAMS

Ansel Adams' quote is important to remember as you search for a photographer. Your wedding photos will be your lasting impressions of one of the most important days of your life. But loving them enough to display and cherish them will depend upon your choice of photographer and his or her input as well as yours. According to The Fairchild Bridal Group (2005), the average cost for wedding photography/videography is $2,570. However, your wedding day is definitely not the time to skimp when it comes to your photography budget. I made that mistake and have regretted it ever since.

I used a professional photographer who was also a friend. His area of expertise was not weddings, yet he assured me it would be fine. In hindsight, I believe it would have been better for both of us if I had hired a photographer with experience in weddings. Your photographer will be intensely involved in your wedding. He or she will be interacting with every one of your guests. The best advice I can give you is to book your photographer immediately after deciding to get married. Well . . . you might want to have a date set first, but you can certainly start interviewing photographers before the date is set. Good photographers are in demand.

> ## Decide on the style of photos you want before choosing a photographer.

So where do you start? Begin your search with word-of-mouth references. But don't just interview one photographer; spend time with at least three. You might even interview one that is above your budget just to compare the style and differences as you determine exactly the kinds of photos that best suit your personality. Just as with the florists, set up appointments to meet with them and view their work. There are basically three types of photography styles to consider: *black-and-white*, *formal/posed* and *photojournalistic* (candid, more natural/ unposed). An unknown author once said, "If you're photographing in color you show the color of their clothes. If you use black and white, you will show the color of their soul."

Personally, I love the candid, more natural style photos. I think they better capture personality and emotion than a formally styled photo. But making decisions has a lot to do with your family and the region where you live. For example, in the South, formal photos are nearly a prerequisite. In fact, a posed, formal photo of the bride is usually displayed at the reception, which often includes photos of her mother, grandmother and other relatives. Your families' expectations for photos should also be considered. My family is happy to simply have one wedding photo to display. Yours may want an entire album. Your future in-laws may desire a simple, candid shot or they may also expect a full photo album. Having a conversation about expectations is important. Most wedding photo packages include an album for the bride and groom and occasionally a photo album for the parents of the bride. But they almost never include a third photo album for in-laws. A photo album can cost around five hundred dollars. If your in-laws would like to have an album, please be sure they understand the costs involved and are willing to spend the money.

As a guest at a wedding, one of the most tedious times can be what seems to be the endless wait for the newlyweds to come out of the church after the ceremony—as they are having photographs taken. One trend that I expect will continue to grow is having the majority of your wedding photographs taken *prior* to the actual wedding day. The photo shoot is scheduled for as much as two weeks in advance. It's a great way to not only eliminate the hassle on your big day but also the luxury of time to capture journalistic photos without pressure. If you are a traditional bride who doesn't want the groom to see you in your dress before the actual ceremony, then consider having all your photos taken except those that would include both you and the groom. For example, you could easily get your family photo, the bridesmaid photos, the groom and his attendants and his family. You could even get your bridal portrait photographed in advance.

> Having photos taken prior to the wedding day is a recent trend.

My friend Patty realized after the photo shoot that she reacted emotionally upon seeing her father and as a result she had blotches on her neck and décolleté in all of her close-up portraits. The photographer did his best to retouch the photos, but she still knows they are there. If you are an emotional bride and don't want all of your photos ruined, consider having at least some of your photo memories taken in advance.

Most experienced photographers can help you compile a list of the most important memories to be captured on film. But it's also a good idea to take the time to plan your own list in advance. To do this, start by simply breaking down photos into a few specific categories, such as *portraits*, *prewedding*, *ceremony* and *reception*. Generally speaking, the *must-have* photos include *the bride*; *the groom*; *the bride and groom; bride and her maid/matron of honor; the bride and her attendants; the groom and his best man; the groom and his attendants; the bride and groom and all of the attendants; the bride with her parents—separately and together* (note: if your parents are divorced, you usually do not include a photo with both of them together); *the groom with his parents—separately and together; the bride and her grandparents; the groom and his grandparents;* and *a photo with the rest of your family, i.e., siblings, aunts and uncles.*

In addition, you certainly want to plan for the *must-have* reception photos as well. They will include: *your arrival at the reception with your new hubby, the receiving line, the bride and groom's first dance, the bride and her father's dance, the best man's toast, the maid of honor's toast, the groom toasting, the bride toasting, the cake cutting and the feeding of the cake, the garter toss, the bouquet toss* and *the two of you leaving the reception.* This is your day, and a beautiful picture is truly worth a thousand words, and then some.

SIMPLICITY MADE SIMPLE

MANY COUPLES ARE CHOOSING TO INCLUDE black-and-white photos, formally posed photos and journalistic photos as part of their memories. The problem might be finding a photographer that is accomplished in all of these disciplines. It might mean hiring more than one photographer.

CONSIDER HAVING A VIDEO MADE of your wedding. A video allows you to record time in motion as well as to capture the voices. This is a great way to have a permanent audio memory of your vows, which is the most meaningful moment of your day. A friend of mine says her grandchildren simply cherish the opportunity to see grandma and grandpa get married. It is their favorite video to watch. If including a videographer seems to be too taxing for your budget, yet you know that chances are you will watch the video more than you will page through a photo album, then perhaps you should choose a smaller photo package instead in order to accommodate both.

TRUST YOUR INSTINCTS. One of the key components of hiring a photographer or videographer is simply liking him or her. If your personalities don't match, don't force it. You will be spending way too much time together. The last thing you want is tempers flaring and nerves screaming.

Check with your church or other house of worship to be sure they allow photos during the ceremony. Today's technology makes it possible to get close-up candid shots from a farther distance. It's also easier to get good photos with less light, which eliminates the use of flashes for most shots. Just the same, **KEEP EVERY ONE CLEAR ABOUT YOUR BOUNDARIES.** You do not want to be distracted in the middle of your vows by catching a glimpse of your photographer. Make clear your expectations—especially concerning photos when your ceremony is in progress.

INQUIRE ABOUT YOUR PHOTOGRAPHER'S EDITING POLICY. A good photo editor will spend quality time tweaking your photos to make them as perfect as possible. Photo processors can easily eliminate red eye and dark shadows and even change the lighting in a photo. My photographer goes one better and offers "plastic surgery" to take a few wrinkles off Mom's face if it makes her feel good. Best of all, it's painless. But it's not free. Because the work is time-consuming, she charges by the hour. I think it's worth every penny for at least a selection of your most important photographs.

Get promised services in writing. Having **A SPECIFIC AND DETAILED CONTRACT WITH YOUR PHOTOGRAPHER IS CRITICAL.** Double-check the contract to make certain it includes the proper date, time and location of your wedding. It should spell out the number of photos, the number of albums, the size of the prints, number of proofs (and whether or not they are an additional cost), the cost of the video and the length of the video. It should also include a date of delivery and overtime costs. Read the cancellation and refund policy and ask to see a business license. Don't hesitate to insist on this; it is important. This will help you defend your contract in case of a dispute.

MOST GOOD PHOTOGRAPHERS HAVE AN ASSISTANT. It is recommended because it saves time in rounding up everyone for photos. Assistants also help to make sure everyone looks his or her best by checking for small details, such as a showing bra strap or other distractions.

> Lord, I pray that in our marriage, my groom and I
> will be vividly aware of moments worth keeping
> in our hearts forever. Alert us to the candid events
> upon which You are smiling. Teach us to look
> for what is noble, pure, lovely, admirable,
> excellent and praiseworthy in each other—for in
> these memories we will enjoy Your peace. Amen.

Gifts: Registry, Giving, Receiving and Sending Thank-You Notes

May no gift be too small to give, nor too simple to receive,
which is wrapped in thoughtfulness, and tied with love.

—L. O. BAIRD

As I researched this topic, I realized how things have changed in the past decade. Ten years ago, it was quite a process to "register" for your wedding gifts. It involved making an appointment with the wedding consultant at a major department store. The consultant would review the store's products with you and write down each item you selected. That information would be logged into the bridal registry book. Those wishing to purchase a gift for you would either need to come into the store and meet with the consultant, or, at the very least, call in and speak with him or her to make a selection. It was quite tedious.

Thank goodness for technology. Today, you simply log in online and start clicking your way toward choosing your desired wedding presents. Of course, you can also register in person. But technology has made that process as simple as scanning your choices into the registry—no more paper and pencil needed. I might suggest, however, before you let your fingers do the walking that you take a little time to think about everything you might need. Most experts suggest starting with the basics before you add the fun dust-collectors that most people never use—you know, like a pasta maker. When, exactly, are you going to find the time to actually make your own pasta? Besides, why would you, with all the gourmet choices available at your grocer today?

> Today, registering for wedding gifts is a fairly easy task.

Basics should include formal dinnerware. Even if you don't plan on using it in the near future, there will be a time when you will truly want to have it. I have spent the last thirty years helping people make their homes beautiful. I can tell you that the older we get, the more traditional we get, and that often translates into having really nice table settings. At some point in your future, you will be grateful for that beautiful china.

You should register with at least two, but no more than four, different stores. Look for stores that have the styles and brands that you most desire. Register a variety of items that allow your guests to be creative in their choices. Also choose items that cover different price ranges so that there is something for everyone's gift budget. Most guests will arrange to have your gift shipped to you prior to the actual wedding day. Carefully think about which address you would like to use for this. Ideally, it would be to a home or office where someone can sign for a gift when necessary. There is a new shipping rule that makes it necessary to sign for "electronics." That covers a broad category of items. Just this week, UPS attempted three times to deliver an item to me; but I was not here. That was the second delivery in a month where I have had to deal with this issue.

IT'S ALSO A TIME TO GIVE TO OTHERS

When it comes to weddings and gifts—it's not all about you. You will also be giving some gifts as well. The wonderful people who have helped you plan and will participate in your wedding should be remembered with a gift. I found it interesting that this tradition dates back to ancient times when Egyptian noblewomen gave precious metals and gems to their ladies in waiting. In the Victorian era, a ring was given to the bride's attendants. Jewelry is still one of the most popular choices for attendants' gifts. My friend Jan had bracelets made from leather and antique buttons. They are not only beautiful, but each was uniquely handcrafted. Traditionally, your maid of honor's gift should be something a little extraordinary. You might consider pearl-studded earrings or even a single small solitaire diamond on a lovely chain for her to wear on your wedding day.

Your groom's attendants should be remembered with a token of your appreciation also. One gift I found recently was a leather travel tie case. It held six ties and also featured a small leather zippered pouch for jewelry and other accessories. Most importantly, you should choose a gift that will be appreciated by the receiver.

You will want to give each set of parents a gift as well. A keepsake or memento, such as a framed poem or a framed wedding invitation along with your wedding portrait, can be a wonderful expression of your love and gratefulness.

Of course, with all the giving of gifts, there should be many thank-you notes written and mailed too. First, let me dispel the myth that the bride and groom have a year to send out the thank-yous. This is not true. You have—at max—two months to get all your *handwritten* thank-you notes sent. Yes, they need to be handwritten. Your guests, on the other hand, have an entire year to gift you with a wedding present. Some guests prefer waiting and giving the gift as a housewarming present instead.

It is permissible to send a prewritten simple acknowledgment first—but, ultimately, you must send a note that specifically mentions the gift and how you will be using it in the future. Traditional rules of etiquette dictate that the bride and groom must do all of this handwriting themselves. However, today, many young brides enlist the help of their maid of honor as well. It is perfectly acceptable to start sending your thank-you notes immediately upon receiving the gifts even if this is months before your wedding.

SIMPLICITY MADE SIMPLE

USE THE SAME MEASURE OF CARE AND DETAIL on your thank-you notes as you did with your invitations. You can use stationery that matches your invitations or you can choose to use something less expensive. You may even add a little humor to your thank-you note styles if it suits your personality.

When registering for bridal gifts, don't forget to inquire about how the retailer maintains their registry. Some automatically update in ten minutes, while others can take as long as forty-eight hours. Obviously, the quicker the update, the less chance of receiving duplicate gifts. **MAKE SURE YOU UNDERSTAND THE RETURN POLICY**—most couples will not get around to returning gifts until after they come home from their honeymoon. If a gift was sent two months prior to your wedding, you will certainly be beyond a standard thirty-day return policy.

Look for a registry that will remain open at least a year. Many offer registry maintenance for two years and some even extend to three years. Also, **FIND OUT IF YOU ARE ENTITLED TO ANY SPECIAL DISCOUNTS** to purchase registered gifts that you did not receive as a wedding present. Most stores will either allow you a one-time shopping spree or give a specific discount on anything you would like to purchase over an established period of time. It is their way of thanking you for allowing them to be your bridal registry.

Here, an overhead covering allows the bride to focus on the beauty of her outdoor wedding without worrying about inclement weather.

Wedding portraits don't have to be posed and formal. Consider taking advantage of the natural beauty or the interesting architecture of your wedding location.

It's the moment you've been waiting for—
being announced for the first time as Mr. and Mrs.

Photograph © Lisette Le Bon/SuperStock

Today—in place of rice—birdseed, flower petals, and bubbles
are often used to send the newlywed couple off in style.

I strongly believe that (1) you may *not* ask guests not to give gifts, and (2) you may *not* ask them to give money or to make a donation instead. This was a problem when Dave and I married because it was a second marriage for me. I already had a home, complete with everything I needed. Most of my friends and family realized that a simple token gift was all that was necessary. But a few members of my husband's family, who did not know me, purchased gifts that I did not need. That did not matter. As Baird's quote above reminds us—no gift is too small or too simple not to be **RECEIVED WITH LOVE**.

Etiquette dictates that wedding gifts should *not* be brought to the wedding reception. That said, many people still feel compelled not to come empty-handed. Be prepared to **HAVE A CARD BASKET AND A GIFT TABLE**, and assign someone to assure that all cards are kept intact with the gift. You don't want to thank Uncle George for a fondue pot when he actually sent you a crystal Tiffany bowl.

> Lord, I am thankful for all the wonderful people whom You have placed in our lives who love us and wish us well. I pray for blessings on all those who share in our happiness and well-being. Amen.

Showers, Brunches and Prewedding Parties

I commend to you our sister Phoebe,

a servant of the church in Cenchrea.

I ask you to receive her in the Lord

in a way worthy of the saints

and to give her any help she may need from you,

for she has been a great help

to many people, including me.

—ROMANS 16:1–2 (NIV)

Nearly the entire sixteenth chapter of Romans is a list of personal greetings, which I found interesting and profound. I believe that it illustrates how important loving fellowship is among all people. Celebrations surrounding weddings give your loved ones opportunities to honor, teach and provide you with material blessings, as well as to offer spiritual support and fellowship to you as a new couple.

"Personal" bridal showers can be a real blessing. The host gathers together a group of married Christian women who have a positive attitude about sex and marriage. They are selected from various stages of life and almost always include a recently married girlfriend of the bride. Their purpose is to encourage the bride-to-be within a Christ-honoring atmosphere. The guests are there to answer the bride's questions, prepare her for realistic expectations and inspire her toward a wonderful married lifetime.

Each of the guests is asked to share one thing she wishes that she had known before getting married. The guests also bear gifts! There are lingerie, bubble bath, CDs to help create a romantic atmosphere, candles, scented sheet spray, massage oil and more! If you are a bride-to-be who would like to be the recipient of a "shower" of this nature, ask a trusted friend.

Traditional bridal showers have also evolved. They are no longer bastions for women only. Many couples are instead opting for a "couple's wedding shower." In the past, the maid/matron of honor hosted the party. Today, almost anyone can choose to host a shower. The only real rule that I think should be followed is that those invited to your bridal shower *must* be invited to your wedding as well. Bridal showers are usually held a few months before the wedding. And although gifts are typically presented, they should not be as prominent as wedding gifts. The real point of the wedding shower is to mix, mingle and have fun. Another new idea for bridal showers that I find quite inviting is a day at a spa. Who can resist a day of pampering? Everyone attending gets signed up for two or three different services. The host/organizer simply makes the reservations and arranges for a lunch where gifts can be exchanged.

THERE'S STILL TIME FOR MORE PARTIES

Wedding brunches are an idea that I really like. A bridal brunch is designed specifically to provide an opportunity for out-of-town guests to renew family bonds and become reacquainted on the day before the wedding. A newer version of a bridal brunch that is becoming popular is held the day after the wedding, rather than before. It is often at the bride's parents' home and extends the opportunity for fellowship time with those we hardly ever see. Since we didn't leave for our honeymoon until two days after the wedding, Dave and I held the brunch at our home. It was wonderful. With most of us still in our pajamas, we simply relaxed with good food and fellowship—it was the perfect "after-the-wedding-day" event.

When it comes to a bachelor or bachelorette party, there is a lot to be avoided. I simply don't understand how what started out as a civilized, black-tie dinner party hosted by the groom's father turned into an opportunity to break all the rules and get drunk. I am grateful that this was not an issue that I had to deal with. And fortunately, good sense is prevailing once again. The latest trends in bachelor parties are weekend-long events involving such things as sports or camping. I like those ideas. I am perfectly content to let my sweetheart spend the weekend biking, fishing, hiking or even fighting it out with paintball guns. Let the men, who want to, put on their camouflage and have a blast. As for a bachelorette party, a second day at the spa sounds just perfect to me.

SIMPLICITY MADE SIMPLE

Remember that **TIMING IS EVERYTHING**. This is especially true when it comes to scheduling a personal "intimacy" shower. It is recommended that it be held two months before the wedding so there is enough time for the bride to deal with potential issues, such as visiting her doctor.

KEEP THE FOCUS ON LONG-TERM, MARRIED INTIMACY as God intends it, if you are planning a personal shower. According to those who shared their stories in *Today's Christian Woman*, "Brides have told them that this turns out to be the encouragement they need to abstain until the wedding night, because the focus is on marriage, not just the sexual experience."

HAVE A *BATH* INSTEAD OF A SHOWER. That's the new term for a groom's wedding shower. A group of guys at one church decided that if the bride could have a shower, the groom should have a bath. The men in the church got together and gave him tools or other "manly" presents. It was a hit.

DON'T FORGET A SIGN-IN BOOK for your shower. As the guests arrive, simply have them make an entry that includes their address and phone number. This will provide the bride with up-to-date addresses and phone numbers. It will make it so much easier when she writes her thank-you notes.

STEER CLEAR OF BACHELOR OR BACHELORETTE PARTIES THE NIGHT BEFORE the wedding. You will be nervous enough without having to worry if your groom is able to get out of bed on your wedding day. I hear those paintball bullets really hurt. Perhaps the weekend before, or at least the night before, the rehearsal is better.

If you have a large family and many friends, **CONSIDER HAVING TWO WEDDING SHOWERS**—one with family and one with friends. The point is to spend time reminiscing, laughing and imparting a bit of wisdom. Your goal is simply to have fun.

> Lord, You are the source of our provision,
> and we have been content with all that You have
> already given us. Yet now You are blessing us with
> even more, and we thank You for meeting all our
> needs according to Your glorious riches. Amen.

PART FOUR

A Day with Your Favorite Friends

Now that you have decided when, where and who will attend, **IT'S TIME TO INVITE YOUR GUESTS**. Wedding invitations will make the first impression of your style. With all the options to choose from, don't feel confined. You can order traditional invitations or design them yourselves. There are wonderful papers available, and I have listed online sources to help simplify your search. A few questions for your caterer are included so that your dining expectations will be met. And remember, stress isn't necessarily negative. The pressure you feel will keep you motivated and energized toward your special day.

And the List Goes On . . .

Now join hands, and with your hands your hearts.

—WILLIAM SHAKESPEARE

Your wedding invitations will be the first impression that your guests have of your wedding style. The stationery, level of formality, tone and detail of your invitation will tell your guests just what to expect. I recently read about a couple that planned a garden-party wedding, making sure that their invitations set the mood. They were informal and colorful. Their plan was a success and they were thrilled when guests arrived in appropriate attire such as sundresses and sandals. It is exactly the response they had hoped for. Finding your style and conveying it via your invitations should be your goal.

The traditional formal wedding invitation engraved in black script on white or off-white paper is still the most popular. It is considered formal in style and includes an inner unsealed envelope. Reception information appears on a separate enclosure in the same font and on the same kind of paper. Additional information, such as a map, hotel options and directions should be mailed separately. It is also appropriate for a formal invitation to include a response card with a self-addressed stamped envelope.

Semiformal weddings can either use a custom-designed invitation or a DIY (do-it-yourself) computer invitation. Homemade invitations have come a long way. Today, there are unusual design kits available—including special ink colors and complete instructions. The quality of the paper is superb and the end result is very impressive. You can create nearly professional looking invitations with beautiful details and embellishments. Do not attempt making invitations at home unless you are a "crafty-creative" person who has plenty of patience and time. If you do not fit this description, but have an acquaintance who would just love to do this for you, then go for it. Be sure that everyone knows and agrees to your deadline. If you choose not to make your own, the Internet is full of good resources where you can select your invitations and even receive a sample in the mail before ordering.

FINDING THE RIGHT WORDS

The wording on invitations has become the more difficult part of creating invitations. Etiquette has put the wordsmith to a challenge for divorced, remarried and other blended families. The traditional standard for an invitation goes something like this:

Mr. and Mrs. Christopher Smith
Request the honor of your presence
at the marriage of their daughter
Samantha Catherine
to
Gregory John Martin
at the Lyndon Country Club
Saturday, the Eleventh of May
Eight o'clock in the evening

If both sets of parents are funding your wedding, the wording should be similar to the following:

Mr. and Mrs. Christopher Smith
and
Mr. and Mrs. James Martin
Request the honor of your presence
at the marriage of their children
Samantha Catherine
and
Gregory John
at the Lyndon Country Club
Saturday, the Eleventh of May
Eight o'clock in the evening

If the bride's parents are hosting your wedding, but would like to include the groom's parents on the invitation, then consider using this wording:

Mr. and Mrs. Christopher Smith
Request the honor of your presence
at the marriage of their daughter
Samantha Catherine
to
Gregory John Martin
Son of Mr. and Mrs. James Martin
at the Lyndon Country Club
Saturday, the Eleventh of May
Eight o'clock in the evening

A DAY
WITH
YOUR
FAVORITE
FRIENDS
125

If you and your fiancé are paying for your own wedding you may choose to do the following (which is what Dave and I did):

The honor of your presence is requested
at the marriage of
Miss Samantha Catherine Smith
to
Mr. Gregory John Martin
Saturday, the Eleventh of May
Eight o'clock in the evening
And afterward at the reception
RSVP

If the bride's parents are divorced, either the parent by whom you were raised issues the invitation or, if they are amenable, both parents may host it together. If they choose to cohost, appropriate wording would be:

Mr. Christopher Smith
and
Ms. Serena Smith
request the honor of your presence
At the marriage of their daughter
Samantha Catherine
to
Gregory John Martin
at the Lyndon Country Club
Saturday, the Eleventh of May
Eight o'clock in the evening

If your parents are divorced and your mother and stepfather are hosting the wedding, then the following wording is used:

Mr. and Mrs. Serena Miller
Request the honor of your presence
at the marriage of her daughter
Samantha Catherine Smith
to
Gregory John Martin
at the Lyndon Country Club
Saturday, the Eleventh of May
Eight o'clock in the evening

If the bride or the groom wishes to honor a deceased parent on their invitation, the following is appropriate wording:

Mrs. Serena Smith
Requests the honor of your presence
at the marriage of her daughter
Samantha Catherine Smith
also daughter of the late Mr. Christopher Smith
to
Mr. Gregory John Martin
Son of Mr. and Mrs. James Martin
at the Lyndon Country Club
Saturday, the Eleventh of May
Eight o'clock in the evening

A DAY
WITH
YOUR
FAVORITE
FRIENDS
127

In addition to invitations and reply/RSVP cards, there are times when you may be sending a separate reception invitation, such as when your wedding date and your reception date differ. And there is also a more recent addition to the wedding stationery repertoire that is becoming very popular. It's the "Save the Date" card. I love this. By letting your guests know far enough in advance that you are planning a wedding, you can be more assured of their ability to attend. It is extremely thoughtful. These early announcements simply make sense if you plan to get married during a holiday or other busy time of year.

They need not be formal, engraved cards. This March, a friend of mine received a "Save the Date" card for a December wedding. It included a magnetic calendar with the wedding date highlighted and was all decked in Christmas holiday sentiment to catch everyone's attention. I will be attending a wedding over Labor Day weekend. I wish they had sent Save the Date cards, because now I have two different weddings the same day from which I must choose.

SIMPLICITY MADE SIMPLE

SAVE MONEY WHEN ORDERING YOUR INVITATIONS by having them printed using the thermography method instead of the engraving method. It costs a fraction of the old engraving method. I used it for the first time for my business cards and was very pleased. It will also give you a much broader range of designs and papers from which to choose.

STICK WITH BASIC BLACK INK to keep your cost down. Foil or colored inks cost more and do not add perceived value. Also, calculate the number of invitations you will need carefully because prices come down drastically for each additional twenty-five you order.

SAVE MONEY BY PRINTING YOUR RECEPTION INFORMATION AT THE BOTTOM of the invitation rather than ordering a separate enclosure.

Be realistic about your ability and time when considering **MAKING YOUR OWN INVITATIONS.** Spend some time perusing samples at printers, stationers and paper stores to get ideas for the kind of style that you want. The simplest way to make your own is by using an "invitation kit." These are available at office supply stores, and I found a much larger selection online than was available through a local store. If you are comfortable with making your own invitations from scratch (and capable in this area), then start with your paper choice first. Again, stationers and office supply stores carry the basics. However, there are several good sources online. Order enough paper to experiment with your layout—that could take several sheets. You will definitely want to have a good paper cutter and perhaps even a paper folder as well. Quick-printing stores will fold or cut your invitations for a small fee.

IF YOU ARE PLANNING A DESTINATION WEDDING, then a "Save the Date" card is absolutely necessary. These cards should be sent at least six months in advance. If it's a busy or holiday season, then I think you need to send them one year in advance. You should also include other details such as hotel accommodations and pricing.

NEVER USE A COMPUTER to address the envelope of your invitation. Envelopes should either be calligraphed or handwritten.

WEDDING PROGRAMS ARE THE EASIEST of all the wedding paper to do yourself. My husband did ours. I located a great option through Polka Dot Design at www.polkadotdesign.com. A simple one-piece panel card that was printable on the front and the back costs $22.50 for a quantity of fifty programs. You can either print them yourself or have them printed by Polka Dot Design. They ship in five to seven days. For a two-piece panel set with ribbon for tying together, the cost was $50.00 for a quantity of fifty.

A DAY
WITH
YOUR
FAVORITE
FRIENDS

129

Lord, I am thankful that the day we have chosen for our wedding is a day that You have set aside as a holy day for us. As that day approaches, may we become more aware of the purpose and love that You intend to be exchanged between us. Amen.

Reception Details

Once in a while, right in the middle of an ordinary life,

love gives us a fairy tale.

—AUTHOR UNKNOWN

I t's time to celebrate your new life together. And how you choose to celebrate is completely up to you and your budget. Your wedding reception, like your ceremony, has its own distinct character. And they do not necessarily need to match. Your original invitation is the key to what your guests are expecting. Meeting, exceeding or falling short of their expectations can make all the difference in whether yours is a time to remember, or a not-so-celebratory affair.

The style and wording of your invitation is all that your guests have when it comes to knowing what to expect. For example, if your invitation was formal and your reception is after 6:00 PM, your guests will expect a formal reception that includes a full-course dinner. Unless you have alerted your guests to a change in tempo, they will arrive at your reception hungry and dressed to the nines. Tipping off your guests to a change in venue is as simple as sending separate *reception* invitations that indicate a change in attire and allow your guests time to return home, eat dinner and switch clothes.

Late afternoon receptions are a perfect way to tame your budget because it is absolutely acceptable to simply serve tea, tea sandwiches and petit fours rather than a full meal. A morning or lunchtime wedding calls for brunch. This meal has the most flexible menu. It may include anything from omelets and pastries to waffles or a serving of beef. If your reception is being held closer to the dinner hour but prior to 6:00 PM, then your guests will be expecting hot hors d'oeuvres. Since food is the most costly portion of your reception budget, making the right choice can make all the difference in whether or not your guests enjoy themselves.

> Traditionally, the time of the reception indicates to guests what type of refreshments or food to expect.

One of your first considerations for the site of your reception should be location. Most brides choose to have the ceremony and reception sites fairly close together in order to keep their guests from having to drive all over town. An important and obvious requirement is making sure that the hall is the right size for your reception. You don't want to overcrowd the space, but you do want to create a festive atmosphere by avoiding having such an expansive area that it overwhelms your guests.

One of the most important things you need to focus on is the value you are getting versus the basic pricing. Some reception halls may have a higher per meal price cost, but may also include all sorts of services that a less expensive place does not offer. You need to know, for example, whether glass barware, china and colored table linens are included or available only for additional fees. The key to determining value is knowing what is important to you. For instance, how important is the overall décor to you? What about the exterior appearance? Do you insist on glass dishes rather than paper or plastic products?

A critically important aspect to consider in choosing a reception site is how you are treated by the staff. *Today's Bride* magazine says, "You should feel that they are truly interested in earning your business, and that they will be both responsible and reliable. If you're going to entrust them with this once-in-a-lifetime event, you need to feel safe that they will do what they say they will do." For more helpful ideas, visit their Web site at www.todaysbride.com.

Whether choosing a sit-down dinner or a buffet, the type of food you select and the number of guests invited will ultimately dictate the price. If you are unsure of which to choose, then start by asking for suggestions and sample a few dishes. Most caterers are more than happy to make this accommodation. If most of your guests will be family and close friends, then a buffet should be fine because the focus will be more on mingling than on dining.

One of the newer developments in serving your wedding reception meal is using *food stations*. I recently attended an event of this nature and I loved it. Each station was placed in a different part of the room and carried a specific kind of food. For example, there was a carving station that included beef and turkey. Another was a pasta station—complete with red and white sauces and a variety of pasta styles. They also had a seafood station. In addition, they had a large salad/vegetable station and dessert buffet set up separately. I like this arrangement because it eliminates the long line at one table and gives folks the opportunity to create their own menu. I started with salad simply because the carving station is where the crowd seemed to be converging while the salad buffet was free of guests.

IT'S FINALLY TIME FOR CAKE!

Some reception halls/caterers include the wedding cake in their package. Be sure to inquire as to whether or not you have to buy *their* cake or if you can bring your

A DAY
WITH
YOUR
FAVORITE
FRIENDS

133

own. If they provide the cake, find out their flexibility in decorating it and also ask to take a taste test. Today's wedding cakes are as unique as the wedding couple themselves. The traditional tiered white cake with the plastic bride and groom is all but extinct. From cheesecake and chocolate Madeira cake to Grand Marnier and poppy seed, the flavors are amazing and endless. But the creativity doesn't stop with taste. Wedding cake decorations now include porcelain bisque and crystal cake toppers, fresh cascading flowers (done by your florist), beads and bows, tulle and lace. You will also find limitless creative choices in design as well as shapes such as hearts, hexagons, squares and circles all teamed up to create impressive balancing acts. As *Today's Bride* says, "The sky is virtually the limit when it comes to today's wedding cakes."

SIMPLICITY MADE SIMPLE

Find out what the decorating limitations may be at your reception hall and when you or your supplier can set up. Also, ask how soon after the reception the decorations must be removed. You should also **CHECK OUT WHICH OTHER EVENTS ARE SCHEDULED FOR THAT DAY** and how much time is allotted between bookings. At the very least, there should be an hour between. Many larger banquet halls use "partitioned" spaces that adapt to the size of the event. If this is the case with your reception site, find out what kind of group will be in the adjoining space. The noise of their party might be an intrusion on your reception. Find out if the hall is covered by liability insurance and if there is an extra charge for security.

Ask about provisions for your musicians at your reception hall. Be sure there is enough room and power for their equipment. (FYI: You will be expected to feed them as well.) While you're checking out things, **DON'T FORGET TO TAKE A TOUR OF THE BATHROOMS** for cleanliness and the parking lot for ease in accommodating your guests, especially the handicapped. Find out if there is a coatroom or valet service available. Will there be someone staffing the office or a building engineer to contact in case you need something during your reception?

ALWAYS INSPECT THE TABLE LINENS. Look at the type of skirting offered for the bridal table, cake table, etc. In most cases, you will pay more for colored rather than white table linens. Inquire as to whether napkins are provided for the cake or if you will need to supply your own. Speaking of cake, ask if there is an extra charge for cake cutting.

Ask your caterer about the amount of time allotted for actual eating. The term "eating" just might include the time to set up and dismantle. **PLAN SUFFICIENT TIME FOR YOUR GUESTS TO ENJOY THEIR MEAL** before the caterer starts cleaning and dismantling. Also ask about the attire/uniforms dress code to be sure it suits your affair. Be sure the staff/guest ratio meets your expectations. If you would like one server for every eight to ten people, then tell your caterer so that your expectation is met. Request that the caterer specify in writing the services they will provide and also spell out what they will not handle.

YOUR FINAL HEAD COUNT will be due a few weeks before your wedding. Once it is determined, it is set. You will pay whether all your guests show or not. Service charges and sales tax are extra, usually around fifteen percent.

IF YOU WILL BE SERVING ALCOHOL, here are a few suggestions and guidelines. To help cut the costs, schedule specific times for serving. For example, a brief champagne toast can be followed by a limited cocktail hour. I chose to serve champagne and allow each guest one additional cocktail. To simply and subtly put an end to cocktail hour, bring out the coffee cart when it's time to serve the cake. You may also choose to serve only beer and wine. It is perfectly acceptable to forgo liquor altogether—especially if you are serving a brunch.

A DAY
WITH
YOUR
FAVORITE
FRIENDS

135

ASK YOUR BAKERY AS MANY QUESTIONS AS YOU LIKE. For example, find out what their delivery policy is and whether they provide a cutting service. When discussing price, know how big they consider a slice to be, since per-slice fees are not necessarily comparable unless you are all talking about the same size piece. If your heart's desire is for a breathtakingly beautiful cake that exceeds your budget, simply order your gorgeous wedding cake in a smaller size for display and then order a sheet cake in the same flavor that can be cut behind the scene and served to your guests. Of course, reserve your date for your caterer and your baker as early as possible since most of the good ones book as far out as two years.

> Lord, what a great feast You have set before us.
> You always provide more than enough.
> As we celebrate with our guests, let us glimpse
> the day that we will also celebrate at
> Your wedding table. Amen.

Dazzling or Stressed Bride—You Choose

He gives strength to the weary

and increases the power of the weak.

Even youths grow tired and weary,

and young men stumble and fall;

but those who hope in the Lord will renew their strength.

They will soar on wings like eagles; they will run and not

grow weary, they will walk and not be faint.

—ISAIAH 40:29–31 (NIV)

I want you and your fiancé to memorize this verse. Why? The answer is simple: You will need the strength of the Lord to get you through the next several months. The closer you get to the wedding day, the more stressed, weary and weak you may feel. You may even feel so stressed that you want to cancel the entire event and simply hide under your bedcovers. Alas, don't be dismayed—it is perfectly natural to experience stress during the wedding-planning process. How you choose to react to stress is the key to surviving this entire chapter of your life without becoming Bridezilla.

The roles were a bit reversed for Dave and me. He was the one turning into *Groomzilla*. He was losing it. He suddenly became someone I wasn't even sure I wanted to have dinner with, let alone marry. My sweetheart simply doesn't deal well with change. And getting married requires several changes, all seemingly happening at the same time. During our dating and courtship, we prided ourselves on the fact that we rarely had a disagreement. We were sure we had a very good relationship. But as we began to combine our lives into one, the pressure also began building. Combining households, dividing up responsibilities, in-law tensions, colliding schedules and simple frustrations caused angry explosions. Because we had not experienced major arguments up until this time, we were not aware of how differently we approached an argument or how well we managed conflict resolution. It was quite the eye-opener.

> It is perfectly natural to experience stress during the wedding-planning process.

Friends and family, of course, offered their opinions on everything, including our newly found disagreements. As the stress continued to mount, their suggestions felt more like demands—which only added to the stress. Suddenly, I realized I was taking everything *personally*. Tears of anger and frustration were washing away what should have been one of the most exciting times in my life. But don't be alarmed by tears; they are a natural release for pent-up anxiety. If you expect stress, I trust you will not be overwhelmed with its presence. (Remember to use the deep breathing exercise I taught you earlier.) Understanding that stress is a natural part of this process is important. Just the same, stress can obscure your joy. Not enough time, fear about finances, fear of walking down the aisle, fatigue, relocation, poor nutrition, change in routine, anxiety, fear of the unknown and relationship tensions all contribute to causing stress. However, stress can also be good for you. Stress can make you feel vibrant, joyful and even motivate by challenging you. It can be positive. It's all in your perspective and attitude.

If you are the kind of person who usually sees the glass as half-empty rather than half-full, prepare yourself. This is going to be a tough time for you. Acknowledge it now and start asking for help and putting together a plan to reduce stress. Consider yourself lucky if your fiancé is an optimist and can coax you through the difficulties and handle most of the unanticipated challenges. If you are hyperactive like me, and get overanxious and wound up over every little setback, then turn to someone who is calm and assuring. This is one area where Dave excelled. He was helpful in giving me perspective and in assuring me that we would work out the details together.

> Acknowledge your stress and start asking for help.

Your stress will not just be emotional; it will be physical too. Planning a wedding is not for the weak. It requires the stamina of Job and the strength of Solomon's army. Attempting to accomplish all the necessary and numerous tasks in a specific amount of time, while simultaneously maintaining your career and meeting all the new social demands are feats to reckon with. Just to complicate things even more, now there are two families who want your attention and have opinions about how well you are or are not doing things.

Add to that the fact that with all these distractions and engagements you are probably not eating properly or you are attempting to lose two dress sizes before the wedding. Regular exercise? What's that? And when was the last time you had a good, full night's sleep? Get ready, because all of this can take its toll on your immune system too. The last thing you need is to fight a three-week cold.

A DAY
WITH
YOUR
FAVORITE
FRIENDS

139

SLOW DOWN AND WORK YOUR PLAN

It's time to get control. First realize that the stress from excessive demands is one of the simplest things to reduce by simply limiting activities. Stop driving all over town and use the Internet and phone to do some of your planning. Stop expecting to find the perfect florist at the cheapest price. Choose what is more important—saving two hundred dollars or saving your sanity. Realize too, that some responsibilities can be delegated. This is where an organized and dependable person is worth her weight in gold. I knew that if I reached out in a cry for help, my friend Jan would do whatever was necessary.

It's also important to differentiate between stress coming from the outside and stress that is self-imposed. For example, if you have not worn a size two dress since you were sixteen, give up on the idea of wearing a size two wedding gown. Also accept the reality that you cannot please everyone—and that includes the two hundred guests you have invited, your soon-to-be mother-in-law and your next-door neighbor. And the most important thing to realize is that there is no such thing as perfection on this earth. So do not expect your wedding day to be perfect. Something can and will go wrong. And that is okay.

SIMPLICITY MADE SIMPLE

USE VISUAL IMAGING to decrease wedding-planning stress. Instead of stressing out over a missed appointment with the caterer, imagine how wonderful you will feel as you walk down the aisle on your father's arm. Envision yourself as a confident, radiant and composed bride who is about to embrace love and joy. Let yourself daydream about all the special things your future will bring.

I HIGHLY RECOMMEND COMBINING WEDDING PLANNING WITH PREMARITAL COUNSELING. Instead of arguing, communicate. My dear Dave had this weird idea that getting engaged and married would suddenly make us function as if we had only one mind and one body. That may seem romantic, but the reality is that I have, and will always have, my own strong opinions and that sometimes they will not match his. Our individual histories and our communication styles along with our unique ways of dealing with stress, anger, disappointment and even joy all played a part in how we managed through the wedding-planning process. Premarital counseling was an enormous help in teaching us useful techniques and giving us perspective.

KEEP A SENSE OF HUMOR. Getting worked up over every little thing is not going to make anything better. Besides, laughter is the best medicine, especially when it comes to dealing with stress. Learn to be flexible. Stuff will happen but it need not cause stress. Keep things in perspective. Yes, your wedding day is a big deal—but it is not the rest of your life. Your marriage is. If something goes wrong on your wedding day, it will not be the end of the world.

TRY SOME PROVEN STRESS REDUCERS suggested by the National Headache Foundation (www.headaches.org). Get up fifteen minutes earlier in the morning. Simplify, simplify, simplify. Recognize that procrastination is stressful. Rather than putting off until tomorrow, do what you can today. Get enough sleep. Allow time for yourself—every day—for privacy, quiet and introspection (and prayer, my addition). Schedule a realistic day. Avoid the tendency to make back-to-back appointments. Do something you enjoy every day. Keep a journal and write down your thoughts and feelings. It can help give you a renewed perspective. Create order out of chaos. Organize whatever space you need to so you always know where things are. Live one day at a time.

Have fun. **TRY DECLARING A WEDDING-FREE WEEKEND.** Do not allow yourselves to talk or argue about anything that involves wedding plans. Take a break and go out with your girlfriends. Sometimes too much togetherness is simply too much. Encourage your fiancé to do the same with the guys. Consider going out on a

A DAY
WITH
YOUR
FAVORITE
FRIENDS

141

formal/fancy date. With all the chaos and hubbub regarding the wedding, it's easy to lose sight of what brought the two of you together in the first place. Get dressed up, make reservations at your favorite restaurant and reconnect. (And don't count the calories.)

Don't forget to **TAKE CARE OF YOUR BODY**. Exercise. Choose the form that you enjoy the most and use it to reduce your stress. For me, Pilates Reformer classes work like a charm. I also get a deep massage whenever I feel the pressure is simply too much. My weakest areas are my neck and shoulders—they are the first places I feel the stress. Be aware of your own trigger points and take care of them sooner rather than later. Or light a few candles and let aromatherapy go to work. Your olfactory system will send signals to the areas of your brain that govern the hypothalamus, which will result in the endocrine and hormonal systems being activated to relieve pain, enhance immunity and make you feel better overall. And don't forget to fix yourself a nice hot cup of chamomile tea as well. Now, relax. Everything is going to be fine!

> Lord, if I am tempted to be anxious, I will put my hope in You. I will remember that my plans are temporal, but Yours are eternal, and You have promised to always be with us. Amen.

Two-Part Honeymoon

Let my beloved come into his garden,

and eat its choicest fruits.

—SONG OF SOLOMON 4:16 (AMP)

Ah . . . you are getting close. Soon you will be able to relax on your dream honeymoon. But before you do, you still have some work and planning to finish up if you are to meet your own expectations for a honeymoon. You may be looking forward to fun, sun and sightseeing, and, of course, you may have high expectations for romantic intimacy as well.

I don't want you to be disappointed, but your honeymoon night may not be your most fulfilling experience. The reality is that like all good relationships, the art of intimacy takes some practice and a lot of communication. Communication is the key. And that means getting comfortable talking about physical intimacy. Many of us are not really good at talking about it.

Sexual intimacy is a most holy form of communication. It will bind the two of you together at the soul. But in order to fully realize all that God meant it to be, we must allow ourselves to be extremely vulnerable. Simply getting married will not necessarily bring you to this level of vulnerability. Over time, as you learn to trust each other more and more, your relationship will become more fulfilling. But you will need to practice. Your honeymoon is the perfect place to begin.

AH, JUST THE TWO OF YOU

Now let's talk about the rest of your honeymoon. Choosing the perfect place for your honeymoon can make your head spin. The first thing the two of you have to decide is what kind of a honeymoon you want. Some couples love a hobby honeymoon. For example, if you both love to hike, sail or play golf, then a hobby honeymoon can be fun. If you love to go sightseeing, then consider a place where neither of you has been before that you can explore together. Some couples want to relax—so a place with warm sun and lots of sand can give you pleasure. Cruises can be fun, relaxing and easy. Of course, you can also choose an all-inclusive honeymoon resort. No matter where you choose to go, realize that honeymoons don't just happen. They too, as the rest of your wedding, need careful planning.

It's also good for you to recognize that travel is stressful. And you have already had a lot of stress just getting to this point. For our honeymoon, we flew off to St. Lucia. We spent three days at a resort, three days sailing and our last day back at the resort. It was perfect because it allowed us to ease into relaxation at the resort before we took on the physical work of sailing. However, it takes a very long time to get to St. Lucia from Lancaster, Pennsylvania. If I could have changed one thing, it would have been not to spend so much time trying to get from one place to the next. This is especially important if either one of you does not travel well.

Both of you have been working hard, your bodies are tired, your heads are spinning and you are just learning how to function as a couple. Be patient and grant each other a lot of grace. You will need to be conscious of each other's limits. Learning to respect limits and separate interests is critical to enjoying this time together rather than arguing about *how* you are going to enjoy the time you have. If you want to go shopping and he wants to scuba dive, try doing as TheKnot.com suggests and simply divvy up the time. "You can watch him swallow seawater all morning, he window shops with you in the afternoon. Don't battle, *balance*."

Each of us has our own unique way of winding down. Some people need a little alone time. Some people need to have the bathroom all to themselves when they brush their teeth or shave their legs. Don't make a big deal out of this. Instead, take a little time for yourself too. Go for a swim, a massage at the spa or take a nap. The main thing is don't push.

SIMPLICITY MADE SIMPLE

Here's a little advice that most doctors recommend. Both of you should have a thorough physical exam before the wedding. This gives you an opportunity to **TALK WITH YOUR DOCTOR** about what to expect and how to prepare for sexual intimacy.

PLAN FOR YOUR TRAVEL. Today, most airlines don't offer much in the way of food. Eat a satisfying, but not too filling, meal before the flight. I always bring a pair of warm socks, so I can take off my shoes and keep my toes toasty.

Keep up your health. I travel a lot and as a result I know how easy it is to catch a cold (or flu) bug onboard. I am recovering from one as I write—so **TAKE YOUR VITAMINS**. I believe in taking extra supplements when I am stressed and/or traveling. I like Airborne, but there are others as well. I start taking them a few days before I travel just to keep my immune system healthy.

A DAY
WITH
YOUR
FAVORITE
FRIENDS

145

Don't be surprised if you catch a case of the post-wedding blues. Lori Seto of TheKnot.com says, **"THE HONEYMOON IS A TRANSITION TIME FOR BOTH OF YOU;** you're tired, you're relieved, you may be nervous (after all, you just tied a permanent knot), and suddenly, after a year of planning, you have all this free time on your hands." You both have a lot on your minds and are emotionally flooded as well. Be patient with each other.

START A PACKING LIST AT LEAST A WEEK BEFORE YOU LEAVE. Find a place where you can start stashing things to pack. I have found the easiest way to be sure I have essentials is to keep a toiletry bag packed all the time. I use it for overnight trips as well as long excursions. That way I don't have to worry whether or not I forgot to pack my hairbrush, sunscreen, makeup remover, etc. Buy duplicates of all your favorites in smaller sizes and tuck them away for travel. One way to keep packing to a minimum is to share some of the basics, like toothpaste, shampoo, etc., with your new hubby.

FIND A TRAVEL AGENT whom you like. And you certainly want a capable agent. But you also want to be able to communicate easily. A good agent will ask a lot of open-ended questions and present you with a range of options. Be up front with him or her about your budget. Give the agent information on all your clubs or memberships, such as AAA auto club or credit cards that may entitle you to a discount. Don't forget your frequent flier points. One way to build up points before your wedding is simply to charge all of your purchases to the one credit card that offers the best (and most) travel points. Of course, don't charge more than you can pay off within thirty days.

IF YOU HAVE RECEIVED BANK GIFT CARDS that you plan to use while on your honeymoon, check their transferability with the bank first. My mother received several bank gift cards at Christmas because all of us knew she would be vacationing the first week of January. Sadly, she discovered while traveling that most of them were not accepted because they were not international cards, despite the fact that they were issued by Mastercard and American Express. To be used out of the states, you must clearly specify "international" at the time of purchase. The bank will exchange the gift cards with international travelers' checks.

Lord, imagining the rest of my life with my new spouse puts the stress of planning in proper perspective. Fill us with the fruit of Your Spirit so that we will be kind to, patient with and faithful to each other as we begin our journey together. Amen.

A DAY
WITH
YOUR
FAVORITE
FRIENDS

147

PART FIVE

A Holy Day of Celebration

YOUR WEDDING DAY IS NEARLY HERE and it's time to battle "wedding jitters." Marriage is a leap of faith, and it is perfectly natural to ask God for confirmation before making a lifelong promise. But keep in mind that most prenuptial anxieties have more to do with the stress of planning than the relationship. So I will discuss how to relieve some of the pressure by choosing someone to help you coordinate the wedding events. Your marriage is a sacred blessing that symbolizes much more than your love. It is an act of worship, demonstrating your obedience to follow God in committed faithfulness to each other. Special consideration should be given to the vows you make.

Confronting Wedding Jitters

If any of you lacks wisdom, he should ask God,

who gives generously to all without finding fault,

and it will be given to him. But when he asks,

he must believe and not doubt, because he who doubts

is like a wave of the sea, blown and tossed by the wind.

—JAMES 1:5–6 (NIV)

By now, you have set your wedding date and have finalized nearly all the plans necessary for your big day. But suddenly, you are having trouble sleeping. You and your fiancé have started to snap at each other, sometimes even arguing over trivial or insignificant things like what color of bath towels or what pattern of china to register for! You are also much more aware of the little things he says or does—or doesn't do. *Why didn't he open the car door for me today? Is that a sign that he will take me for granted once we're married?* This scenario is common to those who suffer from last-minute doubts about whether or not they are making the right decision.

In his epistle to the church, James warned believers not to be *double-minded* (verses 7–8). The Greek word for double-minded is *dipsuchos*, which literally means "two-spirited" or of "two minds," vacillating in opinion or purpose. Wedding jitters, with thoughts of uncertainty, hesitation and fear, can lead you to feel as though you suddenly have two minds. After all, you love each other; you want to be married, and yet, seemingly without warning, these waves of doubt simply come over you. Sometimes they may be so intense that they overwhelm you.

Clinical psychotherapist Dr. Robi Ludwig says jitters leading up to the wedding day are perfectly natural. In fact, some wedding jitters might start the minute your one and only slips an engagement ring on your finger. The reality is that marriage is an immense step. Some realistic anticipation and self-reflection is not only perfectly normal, but is also necessary. Your period of engagement is a time for adjusting to the new life you will be entering. And no life-changing event can happen without going through a natural process of growth.

Serious consideration is part of that process. It is about changing, adapting and letting go of your old life. New beginnings naturally bring about separations and losses. It is a huge decision to commit yourself to someone and make him more important than your own family. But wedding jitters don't necessarily mean you are having second thoughts about the person you are marrying. Robert Butterworth, a trauma psychologist in Los Angeles, says, "The focus is not on the man, but the loss of independence." That certainly is part of it. After all, freedom is precious. Having a measure of anxiety at the thought of giving up your freedom is normal.

> Wedding jitters don't necessarily mean you are having second thoughts about the person you are marrying.

FOLLOW PEACE

So what if you are beginning to think you've got more than a simple case of wedding jitters? What if ongoing anxiety has caused you to lose sleep, and now doubt is affecting your appetite as well? What if you find yourself irritable and impatient with everyone and you really can't stop worrying about whether you are making the right decision? It's time to start asking yourself some very serious questions about the relationship. ForeverWed.com suggests taking some time alone in a quiet place to get in touch with your feelings and your heart.

You need to seek the wise counsel of the Lord. Remember, He gives wisdom generously to those who ask for it. Think about what has changed since you first became engaged. Has your partner changed? Have you discovered something new about him that indicates trouble—like a drug or drinking or financial problem? Is he truly considerate of your feelings? Is he ever physically or emotionally abusive or distant? Is there something about your relationship that you are uncomfortable sharing with family and friends? Being honest with yourself is critically important here because your health and safety may be at risk. These kinds of issues are deal-breakers.

> Seek counsel of the Lord if you are experiencing doubts.

Allowing your family and friends and church to honestly and openly examine your relationship can lead to wisdom you need in deciding whether these are simple wedding jitters or serious issues that make it necessary to call off the wedding. I called off a wedding. My brother called off a wedding. And although in both cases, it was embarrassing and difficult, and it left our fiancés angry, it was the right thing for each of us to do. Fortunately, we both had the support of our family.

My mother was a tremendous help to my brother. She was the only one he felt he could turn to. His fiancée was beautiful, sweet and practically like a sister to all of us. But my brother simply wasn't ready. He made the right decision with the encouragement of my mother. Within two years, his ex-fiancée was married and happily became pregnant soon afterward. No matter how much it hurts or how difficult it is to break off a wedding—the reality is that it gets better—all the way better in time.

Marriage is a leap of faith. If you have both sought counsel and have prayed and believe that you are meant to be husband and wife, then you need to accept the fact that cold feet sometimes simply need a pair of warm "faith socks" to get them through to the wedding day. No matter how well you know each other, the reality is that commitment to each other changes you. Your engagement commitment changed the two of you the moment you said, "Yes." And life together will change after the wedding too. Commitment requires work. Part of that work includes finding a way through the rough spots with faith.

Let's not forget that the stress of planning your wedding also holds some of the responsibility for wedding jitters. There is no reason to feel guilty or bad about your feelings of doubt. The main thing is to talk about them. Talk to your parents, your friends, your minister and your counselor. But also talk to each other about your concerns. You should be able to reassure each other if your doubts are just jitters.

SIMPLICITY MADE SIMPLE

MAINTAIN A SENSE OF SELF. Fear of losing your independence can be scary. But just because you are getting married doesn't mean you have to lose your sense of who you are. Maintain old friendships while expanding your circle of friends. Be realistic when looking at the challenges you face together and separately. Some things naturally will change. But some things will remain the same. The key is to keep the lines of communication open.

Most wedding jitters usually have more to do with the wedding itself than the relationship. Don't be afraid to discuss your anxieties with family, friends and your fiancé. Simply articulating your fears often diffuses them. Once you start talking to others, you will realize that you are not alone. **ENLISTING EMOTIONAL SUPPORT IS CRITICAL** to determining whether you are suffering basic jitters or have serious issues for consideration.

BE AWARE OF THE REACTIONS OF YOUR FAMILY AND FRIENDS. My mother commented many times to me when I was engaged to my first husband that she was concerned that I had stopped doing certain things that she knew I enjoyed. Her fears were well-founded. After twenty years of marriage ended in divorce, I realized that I had compromised myself to an extreme in order to preserve the relationship, and by the time he left I hardly recognized myself.

Don't go through with the wedding simply to avoid the pain and embarrassment it might bring to cancel it. **THE LAST THING YOU WANT IS A HAPPY WEDDING AND A MISERABLE MARRIAGE.** If you have already sent out the wedding invitations, you should send a note to your guests letting them know that the wedding is cancelled. It can be worded as plainly as your original invitation was:

Mr. and Mrs. John Doe
Announce that the marriage of their daughter
Janet Marie
to
Franklin James
will not take place

If time is short and sending a note is not possible, then simply telephone your guests instead. Enlist the help of family and friends in accomplishing this task. And remember, no matter how they may pry, **YOU DO NOT HAVE TO GIVE ANYONE**

AN EXPLANATION. Then return any gifts you have received, including shower gifts, with a note thanking each gift-giver, and explain that the wedding has been canceled.

DOUBTS ARE APPROPRIATE. This is normal, but don't confuse real incompatibility with common wedding jitters. As intimate relationships progress, our differences become more obvious. This can lead to conflict. And although this too is normal, it can be confusing. Understand, once again, that there is no such thing as perfection. Expecting life and marriage to be conflict-free is not realistic. The reality is that even the best-matched couples have areas of differences in communication styles, intimacy, and so on. If you pray, God will either increase your doubts or your peace. If your doubts pass and excitement returns, the key to commitment to each other is learning to expect differences and finding strategies for managing them in your relationship. Look to couples who have not only survived many years of marriage but have also celebrated their differences. Let them be your role models and sources of support.

> Lord, You have promised us peace that surpasses understanding. As we draw near to You, we feel more peace. As we withdraw from Your plan, we are filled with doubt. We choose to follow You even above our love for each other. Give us wisdom and confirm Your blessing on our plans or make clear the path we are to follow. Amen.

The Wedding Coordinator

But everything should be done in a fitting and orderly way.

—1 CORINTHIANS 14:40 (NIV)

My sister's wedding took place in the church with the longest aisle in Cleveland, Ohio. She had a large formal wedding; and as the moment approached for her to walk down that very long aisle, you could see the nervous fear on her face. Then almost on cue, as she took a step forward, the heel of her shoe broke off completely. As the tears began to stream, my brother grabbed the shoe and heel and ran across the street to a gas station where he found glue. Moments later, he returned with the shoe intact. No one saw the last-minute "catastrophe," except those of us in her bridal party; nonetheless, my sister's walk down that aisle was filled with anxiety.

As I have said before, something can and probably will go wrong on your wedding day. Don't worry about it. When and if it happens, let someone else take care of it. For that day, it is not your issue or your problem. Whom do you turn to? Well, unless you have hired a knight in shining armor (like my brother), then I suggest you make sure you have someone assigned to be the "wedding coordinator."

Today, many churches and synagogues have a wedding coordinator on staff. But even if your church doesn't have such an employee, you should assign an individual with wedding experience to help coordinate your big day. The last thing you want to be doing is barking orders to make sure everyone is where they are supposed to be on time. A good wedding coordinator is worth her weight in gold. She will save time and minimize stress for you, your mother and even the pastor or rabbi. She should be completely aware of the location's policies concerning everything from flowers to photographers and videographers to candles and music guidelines regarding weddings. For example, some churches allow video and photos during the ceremony and let those professionals have the freedom to roam about the church. Others do not. Instead, they may want the photographer to remain in the balcony until the ceremony is over. If your photographers are forgetful and start moving about, the coordinator can gently coax them back without a disruption.

> Ask someone to be the "wedding coordinator" to deal with any last-minute needs or mishaps.

The wedding coordinator should know where the best place for the bride is, where bathrooms are located and which guests may have access to them. The wedding coordinator should be familiar with the church's or synagogue's sound system, kitchen, wedding provisions and candle supplies, and the like. In other words, this person should have a good knowledge of where things are and how things operate within the site.

I do a lot of speaking at churches. I can tell you from experience, there is usually a glitch in the program somewhere. Often it is the audio system that causes the problem. For example, just a few months ago, the wireless mikes were nowhere in sight. They were supposed to be left out for us on or near the stage. But instead, they were safely locked away, and no one in attendance had a key to that particular room. After several calls, we finally reached someone who had a key. It took nearly forty-five minutes for him to arrive. In the end, there was yet another problem with the audio system and I had to speak for two hours without being able to get near the podium that held my notes. Every time I approached the podium, an ear-piercing screech surged throughout the auditorium.

Aside from managing the wedding day, wedding coordinators also supervise your rehearsal and guide everyone through his or her part of the ceremony. She will also instruct everyone as to the mechanics involved—such as when to kneel, sit and so forth. Ultimately, her goal is to relieve you of as much apprehension as possible. She should have copies of all your finalized plans, so she is able to make sure that all the details are being taken care of from the moment your day begins.

CHOOSE A SAVVY COORDINATOR

Some suggest simply asking an organized aunt or friend to act as the wedding coordinator, but I don't recommend this. You want all your guests to be able to enjoy themselves and not to have to worry about being responsible for everything going well. Ideally, the wedding coordinator would be someone from the church or synagogue who has keys and access to all necessary areas. If your place of worship does not have a staff member to coordinate the details of the event, then hire someone.

You might even consider hiring a recent bride whose ceremony took place at the same church. She certainly would have inside information and experience to help you coordinate your day. There are also professional wedding coordinators that are usually associated with wedding consultants/planners. If you want assurance as to their credibility, then consider hiring someone who is a member of or who has been trained by the Association of Certified Professional Wedding Consultants. It is a national organization that assures you of having a professionally trained coordinator to help make your wedding day a dream come true. They offer home study and weekend classes for churches and facility coordinators.

Basically, your coordinator should be armed with all essential information and details for your wedding. The more she knows, the more helpful she can be. This is your big day. Don't leave it to chance. The value of a wedding coordinator is peace of mind. The reality is that someone has to be in charge that day and it shouldn't be you. You have already done your part in planning this big event. Today, your job is simply to float on cloud nine, hand in hand with your new husband.

SIMPLICITY MADE SIMPLE

MEET WITH THE WEDDING COORDINATOR early in your planning. She can be a wonderful resource for locating photographers, florists and other professionals. A wedding coordinator will help you through all the necessary church paperwork, including helping you obtain your wedding license. Usually the coordinator will verify your wedding date with the church and arrange for the sound system operator, reserving the date of the rehearsal and the wedding. The coordinator should also be able to provide you with specific information about applicable fees, church facilities and even what the duties of the church custodian are. They should walk you through the church so that you can get familiar with the facilities. They will help you locate dressing rooms and restrooms.

IF YOU ARE HAVING YOUR RECEPTION AT THE CHURCH OR SYNAGOGUE as well, the coordinator should have all necessary information regarding the reception area such as setup and teardown responsibilities and timing.

The wedding processional and recessional are two of the most important elements of your wedding. A wedding coordinator will handle all the logistics of accomplishing this grand portion of your ceremony. She will give last-minute instructions to each wedding party member on how and when to walk down the aisle. The coordinator will help place everyone and oversee how the wedding party enters and exits. Basically, **THE COORDINATOR WILL ACT AS THE CHOREOGRAPHER FOR YOUR CEREMONY.** At the reception, she will work with the musicians and catering staff and can also act as master of ceremonies in helping facilitate the introduction and entrance of the wedding party, the cutting of the cake, the first dance and your departure.

Most **COMPETENT COORDINATORS ARE ALSO PREPARED FOR EMERGENCIES,** as sure to have a needle and thread handy as well as a stain remover kit. One male coordinator said he is probably the only man in the world who walks around with tampons and lip gloss in his pockets.

It is helpful if you **PROVIDE THE COORDINATOR WITH A WEDDING INFORMATION FORM** that includes basic data like the bride's and groom's names; wedding date and time; number of guests expected; the pastor's name; rehearsal date; organist; vocalist; music selections; number of music stands required; and sound system requirements, such as tape, microphone, etc. It should also include the name and phone number of your florist and photographer. If your flowers are to be transferred from the church to the reception, make sure your coordinator is aware of this maneuver so she can assure that it is accomplished.

IF YOU ARE USING CHURCH SUPPLIES such as candelabras, kneeling benches, podiums, candle lighters, candles, etc., give your wedding coordinator a copy of your list with these details so that she can make certain everything is in place when needed.

Your wedding coordinator will help you in deciphering church policy regarding decorations—as to what is permissible, and when you may start decorating and when the decorations need to be removed. Your church may require approval of music prior to your wedding. The coordinator can handle this as well. You should **ASK FOR A COPY OF THE CEREMONY GUIDELINES** for your church. For example, if you want communion administered, most churches require advance notice.

DISCUSS HOW YOU WANT TO HANDLE A RECEIVING LINE with your coordinator. Depending on the size of your wedding, a receiving line can get to be quite tedious for you and your guests. Today, many couples are choosing to hold the receiving line until the reception rather than detaining guests at the church. If you choose to do this, then let your guests into the reception hall first. After everyone has had a chance to hang their coats, use the restrooms, etc., then you can initiate a receiving line.

> Lord, when our wedding day finally arrives,
> please bless the events of the day with Your
> grace to keep everything in order.
> Let us be aware of Your presence. Amen.

A Sacred Ceremony

For this reason a man will leave his father and mother
and be united to his wife, and they will become one flesh.

—GENESIS 2:24 (NIV)

Nothing suggests a bond more than the words "they will become one flesh." The bonding of two people in marriage is covenantal. God used the depth of His own commitment to Israel as an illustration of a covenant when He said, "as Christ loved the church and gave up himself for her" (Ephesians 5:25). The covenant of marriage is a biblical framework designed to enable the husband and wife to respond to each other with a deepening love in a trusting relationship. Only the biblical concept of marriage as a lifelong covenanted commitment, nurtured by love and intimacy, can provide such a completely safe environment for love to grow.

So how does this parallel of Christ's loving the church affect your marriage ceremony? Obviously, the promises made and words spoken should be Christlike. But how do we express this? First, we must recognize that God created marriage and He made the person who will be your lifelong companion. In addition, according to

Malachi 2:14, God is the primary witness to our covenant to each other. Of course, God is the ultimate example of covenanted loyalty. Therefore, although our society says this is the bride's day, in reality it is God's day. It is God Who is honored when a couple commits themselves to loyalty and purity in their new life together. Simply translated, a wedding ceremony is, in fact, a worship ceremony.

> A wedding ceremony is, in fact, a worship ceremony.

The most important consideration, therefore, should be to examine every element of our ceremony to assure that it does not trivialize the significance of the covenant, relationship or the worship. For example, music is one of the most powerful elements in worship. It can bring us to our feet or take us down on our knees. When choosing music for your ceremony, the overall sentiment should be one that demonstrates Christlike compassion and enduring love in a way that is appropriate and leads people to worship. That does not mean that no secular music can be chosen. It just means that the lyrics should at least symbolize Christ's compassionate love. They don't have to mention Christ to accomplish this. There is plenty of poetry and other creative expression within the Bible that doesn't actually mention Christ. But it does express the attitude of Christ's love and loyalty. That is the key. If there is a secular song that is significant to the two of you that creatively symbolizes such expression, then use it.

HEAVEN AND EARTH REJOICE OVER YOU

Just as the Israelites sealed their covenants with the holy name of God—Yahweh—so too your marriage covenant will be sealed in God's name. That means He is present. God represents heaven; your guests are witnesses of earth, making heaven and earth witnesses to your marriage. Some might call this a "cosmic" event. That's pretty amazing when you think about your marriage in the scheme of God's plan for mankind. Because your wedding is a significant, cosmic event, nothing should trivialize it.

When we meditate on the covenanted promises in the Bible, we read very little about how everyone was dressed or what they ate afterward. It's not even the location or the decorations that are the focal point. No, it is the promises themselves—the vows —that hold center attention. It is the speaking of the vows before God and others that is the reason for this event. Your guests, particularly your bridal party, are witnesses who in the eyes of God are also making a promise to commit themselves to encouraging you, praying for you and even providing a level of accountability for the two of you.

Weddings are clearly a time of celebration. And joy should be the prevailing mood. Ken Essau, who teaches Old Testament and marriage and family courses at Columbia College, Abbotsford, British Columbia, says, "The joy should come from the event and not from the extravagance of the flowers, location or reception, though all these can add to the enjoyment. Ideally guests should remember the strength and maturity of the couple as they committed themselves to one another and praised the awesome God Who brought them together. Simplicity is more likely to keep the focus of the celebration on people and God rather than on the less important."

As you think about personalizing the design of your wedding ceremony, focus on allowing it to be an expression of worship. Let it also reflect joy, celebration, respect, dignity, the attending community and love. Let your primary goal remain simple: The central component of your ceremony will be your solemn, eternal covenant with each other and God. Let your wedding service be a testament to your life and your faith in Christ.

> Let your wedding service be a testament to your life and your faith in Christ.

SIMPLICITY MADE SIMPLE

The marriage ceremony generally lasts about thirty minutes. **HERE IS A GENERAL OUTLINE** for you to use to organize your thoughts for your ceremony.

- ➤ Seating of the honored guests (parents and grandparents)
- ➤ The bridal procession
- ➤ The giving of the bride in marriage
- ➤ Welcome and invocation (you may want a call to worship here instead)
- ➤ Wedding address/sermon
- ➤ The marriage pledges
- ➤ Exchange of rings
- ➤ Prayer—blessing of rings
- ➤ Unity candle
- ➤ The pronouncement of marriage
- ➤ Lord's Prayer
- ➤ Benediction
- ➤ Couple's kiss
- ➤ Introduction of new Mr. and Mrs.
- ➤ The recessional

Discuss your visions for your ceremony with your fiancé. **CONSIDER ALTERING OLD TRADITIONS OR SIMPLY ADDING SOME NEW ONES** that represent your own individuality. Often symbols or symbolic actions were used to accent the significance of a biblical covenant. The concept of symbols easily translates to a wedding ceremony. The unity candle ceremony is symbolic of two families joining together. Traditionally, there are three candles. Each of your mothers lights one of the side candles. Then the bride and groom take one of those lit side candles and light the center candle together. You can either extinguish the side candles or allow them to continue burning as a symbol that your individual personalities will continue to be different and equal, while committed to each other and to serving God.

REMEMBER THAT THIS IS NOT A PERFORMANCE. It is an act of worship. God is present. As you consider your music selections, prayers and readings, let them affirm your faith and speak to your guests about your personal convictions. One way to personalize your ceremony is simply to include favorite poetry, literature or original music.

One idea is to **INCLUDE A PARENTAL BLESSING** that has biblical roots. I find this especially significant as an element of a Christian wedding ceremony. It is quite powerful to hear the bride's and/or groom's fathers pray a blessing over them. Blessings can also be offered through songs or simple heartfelt words of appreciation from family and friends who want to pray for you.

MAKE IT AN INTERACTIVE CEREMONY. Guests usually are expected simply to be spectators. However, there is no reason why you can't transform your ceremony to include participation. You can call upon guests as a group to give their promise to support you or you can have individuals act as representatives for the whole gathering— allowing them to offer their blessings by reading appropriate Scripture, poems or prayers. This is the perfect way to include children from a previous marriage in your ceremony.

CONSIDER USING A METAPHORICAL IMAGE TO CREATE A LASTING IMPRESSION of your union. You might decide to share a glass of wine and another of bitters—a visual image of your agreement to share life's joys and sorrows. Many cultures use the tying of the hands with a ribbon as a visual image of your souls being bound together in life. A strong visual image of your covenant commitment might be the signing of your names on a parchment or at the front of your Bible together. If you are both gifted with singing voices, consider sharing a song. Naturally, the sowing of seeds is a good analogy of how you expect your marriage to grow. You could demonstrate this simply by planting seeds or seedlings in a pretty container. Your parents could even contribute by sprinkling your seeds with water.

CONSIDER A DOUBLE WEDDING. It's twice the fun and nearly half the price. Sisters or even close friends might want to make a double ceremony. Each bride still has her own maid of honor, though they often act as each other's honor attendants. They usually share the rest of the attendants. They may or may not decide to dress alike. But their attire should complement each other's. And the brides do not have to dress like identical twins. Their dresses simply must be of the same level of formality and length. All male members of the wedding party would dress alike. Who walks down the aisle first? Usually this is solved by allowing the eldest bride to go down the aisle ahead. Everything but the vows are read only once. Both grooms and their best men enter together. Both sets of ushers, paired by height, lead the processional. The female attendants of the first bride enter followed by the bride and her father. The second bride's attendants and the bride and her escort then proceed down the aisle. If the brides are sisters, a close relative usually escorts the second bride down the aisle. But her father gives her away.

> Lord, we desire to bring meaning and purpose
> to our ceremony. We do not want to include vain
> repetitions of ritual that we do not understand. Please
> give us a fresh perspective on the symbolic acts of wor-
> ship that our union represents. Let Your glory shine
> through us and through our words. Amen.

Your Wedding Vows

At the touch of love everyone becomes a poet.

—PLATO

The Hebrew word that means "to speak" and "to say" is often translated in the Old Testament as "to promise." In other words, to give your word to someone was to make a promise. The entire Bible integrates the theme that God has given His Word, or His promise, to bless those who simply believe in Him as Abraham did. The apostle Paul wrote about God's covenanted commitment to Abraham in Romans 4:20–21, noting that Abraham's faith-response to God's *statement of intent*—calling it a promise—"did not waver through unbelief regarding the promise of God, but was strengthened in his faith and gave glory to God, being fully persuaded that God had the power to do what he had promised." The Greek word translated as "promise" of God in Romans 4:20 is *epaggelia*, which implies an announcement or pledge: "especially a divine assurance of good."

Marriage, family and child therapist H. Norman Wright wrote in his book *The Complete Book of Christian Wedding Vows*, "Promises have a future quality about them as well. A promise is only kept when it's fulfilled." We can *say* anything, but our words are meaningless until we actually act on our promise. Keeping a promise is a lifelong task, just as God's promises are eternal.

During my devotions this morning, I read about a Christian couple who decided to take salsa dancing lessons. I found it interesting: First, because my husband and I are about to take two classes ourselves (I won them at a silent auction); and second, because I do believe that marriage is much like a dance, requiring cooperation and communication.

> Marriage is much
> like a dance;
> it requires cooperation
> and communication.

This couple wrote about the marriage lessons they learned through salsa dancing. Their instructor began, "Ladies you always start with your right foot. You can remember this because *women are always right!*" (Just what every woman wants to hear.) But as in the dance of life, being right requires you to know when you are wrong and to admit it. For example, you are wrong when you mistakenly start off the salsa on your left foot, and making a disrespectful comment to your husband is akin to starting off on the wrong foot. If the wife is to be a helpmate in the decision making, then she needs to know when she is wrong and to humbly admit it.

In ballroom dancing, the man always leads. The man's first step is with his left foot. But if he is to be a good leader, then he needs to be a good communicator and signal to his partner before moving forward with the next dance move he anticipates. For example, he can't, without warning, grab his partner's arm and expect her to gracefully spin. She needs to know in advance what he expects of her in order for her to do it gracefully. That means discussing it verbally or through some other method of communication. In the case of dance, the method is a simple touch; in life, he must learn to express his expectations clearly.

The promises you make during your vows are more than words—they are indicators of what each of you will expect from your marriage. In dance, you use your body movement to indicate what you expect of each other. In marriage, your vows will be your indicators of your next dance step together.

H. Norman Wright says, "The language of a wedding service should be the language of promising. That's why the ceremony has such a serious ring to it. The promises are to be spoken seriously and without coercion. And once you make these promises through the exchanging of vows, you and your spouse will never be the same. You will move to a new life status by virtue of your promising. A transformation will take place. What was separate before will now become 'one flesh.' And no matter what happens, this fact can never be erased."

> Your vows are more than words— they indicate what each of you expects from your marriage.

MAKE A PROMISE

Now that you understand the significance of your vows, let's talk about exactly what you want to say. One of the most popular ways for people to customize their weddings is by writing their own vows. Although this is by no means a requirement, there is no reason to be afraid of trying it either. It can be a wonderful experience in communication for the two of you that may continue to be a catalyst for future communication. I have always found it much easier to express emotional thoughts through writing rather than speaking because it protects the listener from the distraction of my physical expression of emotion. It also helps me focus and remain clear in what I want to convey.

Therefore, I suggest that the first thing you do before actually writing your vows is to write a love letter to each other. The goals should be to elaborate, get mushy, go deep and be creative. Tell him why you love him and what you enjoy most about him. Reminisce about when you first met and first fell in love. Write about how you knew he was the one. Remind him of a few of your best and favorite times together. Reflect on specific Scriptures that you have shared or even songs that you consider "yours." Just let it flow. Then give these letters to each other and read them while in each other's presence.

Then simply wait for each other's reactions to the words you have written. Pay attention to those statements in the other's letter that you find particularly heartfelt. Focus on them because they are the key trigger points to writing your vows. These expressions and words of love will be the foundation for what is meaningful for the two of you, and hearing this deeper exchange will make writing your vows much easier. You may also learn something about how best to express love to your fiancé by the way he expresses it to you. For example, some people are verbal and need spoken affirmations of love. Others are tactile and appreciate a hug or the touch of a hand more than words. This information will be valuable for your marriage, forever.

SIMPLICITY MADE SIMPLE

Remember that you are not alone at your wedding. Leah Ingram, author of *Your Wedding Your Way*, says, "In writing wedding vows, you have to keep in mind that you're addressing more than just your partner. You're also addressing the people attending the wedding, and that may entail friends, family, work colleagues and even strangers." **VOWS SHOULD BE APPROPRIATE** for your audience. That may mean avoiding metaphors that border on "more information that I needed to know." Strive to find a balance that is dignified, yet personal.

KEEP YOUR VOWS IN LINE WITH THE STYLE OF YOUR WEDDING. If your wedding is formal in nature, then your vows should also be more formal. Lilting harmonies from your favorite pop song would not be suitable. I read about one bride who should have thought twice before saying, "You're the chocolate on my ice cream sundae." It was a childish comment in the perspective of her otherwise formal wedding. Nevertheless, she gets an honorable mention for natural exuberance!

Remember that you are not writing a book. **TWO TO THREE MINUTES IS THE IDEAL LENGTH FOR YOUR VOWS.** Twenty minutes is a lecture, not a promise. If you can't get them edited down to a respectable few minutes, ask your maid of honor to help.

GET APPROVAL BEFORE YOU MEMORIZE YOUR VOWS. You absolutely want to have your pastor/officiant read your vows before you begin learning them to make sure that they are in keeping with faith's doctrine.

PRACTICE SAYING YOUR VOWS. But don't forget to write them down as well. No matter how perfectly you think you have them memorized, trust me, on the day of your wedding you may find it difficult to think, let alone speak. I always write my lecture notes on my computer using a font size of fourteen so I don't have to squint to read them. This is also helpful for reading through tear-filled eyes. Just let your maid of honor hold your script in case you need a little prompting.

DECIDE IN ADVANCE whether you want to share your promises of love with each other before the wedding, or whether you want to surprise each other. If you choose to surprise each other, then at least specify a word count so that one of you doesn't overwrite the other, which can be embarrassing. About sixty to one hundred words each is a good goal. You may also choose to read your vows together or in alternating statements. For example, *I (bride) from this day forward promise to be there for you. I will share in your joys and your sorrows, standing by your side through whatever life brings our way. From this day forward, I (groom) promise to* *live with you and grow old with you. I promise to do all I can to keep our marriage strong and happy and alive with possibilities. Etc.*

Lord, may the vows that we make on our wedding day be strong enough to hold us together when storms blow or when natural light dims our view of each other. Write our promises on our hearts so that we will always remember them, come what may, and enjoy the covenant of love that You designed our marriage vows to create. Amen.

God's Plan for
Your Marriage

Submit to one another out of reverence for Christ.

—EPHESIANS 5:21 (NIV)

As you are about to begin your marriage, let's consider the ballroom dance class for a few more instructions. Marriage and dance have the same requirements; two people, one who leads and one who follows. But they also require a choreographer, designing and instructing them from behind the scene as to what steps they should take and when they should take them. The choreographer chooses the dances and even the music.

When you watch two people dancing, you see two people working together in harmony. Now imagine for a moment if they each ignored the plan of their choreographer and decided to each go his or her own way. How do you think the dance would appear? It would probably look like a train wreck with each of them stepping on the other's toes. One of them may even tumble to the ground after a near-miss collision—it would not be a pretty sight.

The same potential mishap is true for your dance of marriage if you choose to ignore the plans of your marriage choreographer—God. He gives us specific instructions for creating a good marriage. This is His choreographed dance—you are simply the chosen dancers.

Building a God-centered marriage is critical to creating a good marriage. The more we know Him, the more we learn that He knows what is best for us. God desires for us to grow and have fulfillment in marriage. That is God's ideal for marriage. But unless we are growing in our knowledge of Him, we cannot grow properly in our partnership with each other. Unless we know, speak to and listen to our Choreographer, we will not learn the dance of marriage.

> Building a God-centered marriage is critical to building a good marriage.

God wants the best possible marriage for the two of you. But He does not promise that marriage will be blissfully perfect or without problems. The two of you are unique individuals who have been reared in different families. No matter how similar your backgrounds may or may not be, the reality is that meshing together in unison can be a bit traumatic. The reality is that neither of you is custom made. It takes time to learn to fit together.

It takes time to learn the dance steps, so don't be disillusioned or doubt your bond simply because you find difficulty in coming together as partners in the dance. Remember that this life is a refining process, and you may see a few sparks flying as your Choreographer fine-tunes and polishes your marriage. You can be thankful that grace and mercy are two very important gifts from God to strengthen us as we practice the dance. But these are also gifts that we need to offer to each other. In fact, few marriages survive without grace and mercy.

Most of us understand grace pretty well. Grace is a state of sanctification that we enjoy because of God's willingness to forgive us. Mercy is God's compassion in choosing not to judge us even when we deserve to be judged. It is a blessing that is an act of divine favor. None of us is perfect. Without God's gift of grace and compassionate mercy, we would all be doomed. The same is true for marriage. Unless we choose to offer grace and mercy to each other, there is no way we will be able to dance in harmony. We must be willing to forgive and even forget when our partner steps on our toes.

God ultimately wants you to develop intimacy. Your dance should express a deep and abiding passion for each other. In marriage, you should be able to express your deepest passions. The apostle Paul recognized God's design of sexual passion and encouraged us to express it appropriately for each other when he said, "Do not deprive each other except by mutual consent and for a time, so that you may devote yourselves to prayer. Then come together again so that Satan will not tempt you because of your lack of self-control" (1 Corinthians 7:5). This verse encourages us to be intimate, but more importantly it encourages faithfulness.

Faithfulness is both an attitude and an action. When you are faithful to one another, you avoid even the temptation of adultery, and you never give the appearance of interest in another person. Ed Wheat, MD, and author of *The First Years of Forever*, says, "Faithfulness is not only an ongoing choice. It is a continuing call to action. If you don't express it, if you don't demonstrate it in your daily life, it can't be faithfulness."

How do we demonstrate faithfulness? Understanding the love language of your partner and knowing what really matters to him is key to demonstrating love and faithfulness in a way that your partner will most easily understand and respond to. It is amazing how powerful unconditional love and acceptance are. They are life changing.

Drs. Gary and Barbara Rosberg said in their book, *The Five Love Needs of Men and Women*, "Your response, initiative and connection to your husband are crucial to the health of your marriage and family. Your expression of your unconditional love and acceptance is the very force that will drive you together in the midst of the testing time in your marriage." The hard part is being able to offer unconditional love and acceptance, even when your partner makes poor decisions or when he disappoints you. But without your offer of love and unconditional acceptance, your marriage will tear apart.

My friend Dr. James Hanna is an amazing counselor and author of several books. In his book, *Intimacy: The Quest for Life Connections*, he says, "A relationship requires sustained commitment to understanding another person, not only with one's mind but also with one's heart. It means appreciating differences and tolerating times of boredom and lessening interest, desert periods of diminished emotion. It involves identifying, expressing and containing boundaries between 'I' and 'we.' It requires creating a safety zone where the other person can come without fear of judgment and criticism so that feelings, thoughts, hopes and fears can be freely exchanged."

> Your marriage should be the one place where both of you feel free and safe to express your inner emotions.

Your marriage should be the one place where both of you feel free and safe to express your inner emotions. Sharing your sadness, fear, joy—all emotions—is a way of connecting with the inner being of each other. That sometimes takes courage. It requires vulnerability. James Hanna says one of the barriers to building such a soul connection is the difficulty that we sometimes have in identifying our feelings. For example, it's often easier to recognize anger while being unaware of our sadness. Unless we recognize our true feelings, we cannot express them. Instead, we may demonstrate anger when, in fact, we are simply sad. That's why it makes sense to take time before attempting to express ourselves. Waiting until we are sure which emotion we are feeling may be the most positive thing we can do for our relationship. Spending time with God in prayer and reflection before we put on our dancing shoes is a very good warm-up exercise for the dance of marriage.

SIMPLICITY MADE SIMPLE

THINK ABOUT HOW YOU WANT TO EXPRESS YOURSELF. When you are angry or hurt, you need to express your emotions in a way that will enhance your relationship, rather than diminish it. Hanna says, "An intimate relationship accommodates the stranger in ourselves and in others." Simply realizing that sometimes we are strangers even to ourselves is important to understanding our emotions. Sometimes I am not able to pinpoint what is bothering me. Not knowing or understanding the cause is fine. The problem is when I act on those feelings in a negative manner toward my husband when he has no part in the reason for my feelings. What I am feeling at that moment may have nothing to do with him. He shouldn't take the brunt of my frustration, anger, whatever, simply because he happens to be within firing range.

Communicate. Learn your love language of affirmation and use it to communicate. I need my husband to communicate to me with touch. A simple hug or hand on my shoulder reassures me. **SEXUAL INTIMACY IS NOT POSSIBLE WITHOUT GOOD COMMUNICATION.** The ebb and flow of sexual intimacy requires emotional honesty and direct communication as well as physical contact. If my husband neglects touching me throughout the day, it's difficult for me to feel connected to him in a sexual way at the end of the day.

Affirm each other. It's so easy to do—yet so easy to forget. Mark Twain once said, "I can live a whole month on one compliment." Imagine how amazing your marriage could be if you simply **LET THE COMPLIMENTS FLOW.** Men in particular respond to basic affirmations. "I'm proud of you," "You are my best blessing" or "I feel safe with you" are simple statements that are key to your unconditional love.

SHOW GRACE. ALL OF US NEED IT. But sadly, we need it most when we are least aware of the need for it. It's when we are acting badly, making mistakes or simply being selfish that we most need grace. It's also when it is hardest for our partner to administer it. If my husband is disappointing me, the human side of me wants to let him have it! But God calls on us to be Christlike and to express grace—sometimes an extra dose of grace. As my husband's wife, it's my job to cover him in grace if he needs it. That means forgiving him over and over again. It means encouraging him when life's pressures are building up. It means standing by him when he is experiencing or feeling failure. Whenever you are tempted to let your temper fly, remember that you love your spouse. Remember how important forgiveness is. Remember that Christ forgave you.

Commit to praying and studying God's Word together. **COMMIT TO GROWING SPIRITUALLY**. During your dating years you both made it a priority to schedule time together. It's easy to assume that once you are married, you would spend more time together. But often when schedules begin to collide, it is actually harder to spend time together unless you continue to prioritize and schedule it. While you were engaged, you probably made it a priority to pray about most things together. You may have attended Bible study together. Those practices not only need to continue but also will be essential to the health of your marriage.

> Lord, we are thankful that You lavish us with grace and mercy. You give us grace, unmerited favor, to accomplish what we cannot do alone, and You give us mercy to cleanse us from the bondage of our mistakes. Keep Your grace and mercy upon us, and let it abundantly overflow in our love for each other. Keep us in the palm of Your hand, as we hold on to each other. Amen.

Conclusion

Your wedding day is drawing closer. I hope you and your fiancé have established your priorities and have learned the art of flexibility. I pray that you have learned the difference between outside stress and self-imposed stress. You may not be able to control all the stress, but you can decide how you choose to respond to it. Your emotional reaction to issues is often more important than your actual decisive response. You will find that people are more willing to listen to and accept your viewpoint and your choices when they are presented lovingly instead of as a demand.

Don't let yourself get overwhelmed. Instead, use this planning process as a way of gaining communication and tact skills. They will serve you well through all your days of marriage. Set aside quality couple time to simply enjoy each other without worrying or fretting about wedding plans. Remember, it makes no sense to have planned the perfect wedding if you don't survive the plans as a couple.

I hope you have sought out positive mentors and spiritual counsel as you move forward to your wedding day. While you're at it, you might also consider taking some dancing lessons. They will come in handy as you move toward the dance of marriage. Your Creator is already choreographing your steps—study His design well.

And think carefully as you craft your vows. The promises you make are more than words. They are indicators of what each of you will expect from the other throughout your relationship. Building a God-centered marriage is critical to building a good marriage. Accept your differences in communication and intimacy styles while finding strategies to manage them effectively in your relationship. Practice grace and mercy—extend them often and in abundance to each other. They are critical for establishing harmony in your life together.

Go in peace and celebrate your new life together.

Many blessings on your head,
Sharon

Bibliography

Hanna, Dr. James W., Intimacy: *The Quest for Life Connections* (Cleveland: United Church Press, 1992), 62.

Hawxhurst, Joan C., *Interfaith Wedding Ceremonies* (Kalamazoo, Michigan: Dovetail Publishing, 1996), 12.

Holmes, Kelly, "Getting Personal—Bridal Showers with an Unexpected Twist!" *Today's Christian Woman* (January/February 2006), 34–36.

Ingram, Leah, *Your Wedding Your Way* (Chicago: Contemporary Books, 2000), 95.

Woodham, Martha A., *Wedding Etiquette for Divorced Families* (Chicago: Contemporary Books, 2002), 209.

www.drdaveanddee.com

www.mbconf.ca

www.tommynelsononline.com

The Spirit of Simple Living®

by Sharon Hanby-Robie

A Simple Wedding

The Simple Home

A Simple Christmas

The Spirit of Simple Living series offers uplifting titles that will help readers create a style of living that combines beauty and functionality with faith and spirituality. Join author Sharon Hanby-Robie as she shares inspiring narrative, real-life examples and expert tips on how to live in the true spirit of simplicity.